SOUL
CONSCIOUSNESS

SOUL
CONSCIOUSNESS

A New Vision of Community
Empowerment and Cultural
Transformation

Stephen Vick

Library of Congress Control Number:		2017917976
ISBN:	Hardcover	978-1-5434-6796-3
	Softcover	978-1-5434-6795-6
	eBook	978-1-5434-6794-9

Print information available on the last page.

Rev. date: 10/27/2018

To order additional copies of this book, contact:
Xlibris
1-888-795-4274
www.Xlibris.com
Orders@Xlibris.com
769602

CONTENTS

Foreword   Sam Chaltain vii
Preface   Stephen Vick..ix

Chapter 1   Roberto Carlos Rivera, Chicago, Illinois............................1
Chapter 2   Does the Soul Contain Melanin? 14
Chapter 3   Loren Fardulis, San Diego, California 22
Chapter 4   Holy Sparks Revealed 36
Chapter 5   Charles Perry, Mississippi and Washington DC 42
Chapter 6   A Faith-Based Approach 51
Chapter 7   Jewel Ware, Chicago, Illinois...58
Chapter 8   Seeking Out and Deleting Files 66
Chapter 9   Teh' Ray "Phenom" Hale Sr., Chicago, Illinois 70
Chapter 10 Voices of a Nation 84
Chapter 11 Anndrea Miller, Chicago, Illinois 91
Chapter 12 An Inclusion Policy to Support Systems Change.............104
Chapter 13 Antwan Diggs, Buffalo, New York....................................111
Chapter 14 Transformational Leadership 122
Chapter 15 Mariana Osoria, Chicago, Illinois 129
Chapter 16 Learning to Breathe...139
Chapter 17 Volney "VP" Parker, Little Rock, Arkansas 143
Chapter 18 A Final Thought...156

Soul Consciousness 159

This book is dedicated to my wife Marlene, my
three children Camila, Alex and Olivia
and in memory of my father, Nicholas A. Vick

FOREWORD

Sam Chaltain
Washington DC

Steve Vick is one of those people.

You know, the kind you meet and want to hold on to forever, the kind you feel honored to know, the kind that show you, through their words and actions, what it means to be alive, what it means to embody deep principle, what it means to lead.

It makes sense then that when Steve would decide to write a book, he would do so in a way that would elevate the stories of other people like him—other souls whose own ways of being in the world have provided their own forms of harbor light to the rest of us. *Soul Consciousness* is a book about people discovering the power and uniqueness of their own voice. It is alive with spirit, sadness, persistence, and triumph. It is the beginning of a lifelong path we must all take up and complete by walking, and it is the sort of thing that only Steve could make manifest in the world—because only Steve is so directly connected to so many other similar spirits, each pursuing their own path to discover what it is that makes us most distinctly human.

Consequently, *Soul Consciousness* is a book that will remind you, in this era of political fecklessness and amorality, where our most potent power as a people truly resides. As Steve puts it, "Most communities contain the answers to many of their own challenges. It is only from within each community and through those who are closest to the problem can the real creative solutions be found."

"In order to effectively address community challenges," Steve argues, "there needs to be a deeper consciousness and purpose toward understanding our collective human condition." This book, these people—*these lives*—come together to form a loving tribute to all of us in search of deeper meaning, deeper connection, and a deeper sense of wonder. If you read it closely, it will change you—just as Steve has surely changed for the better all of us who have been fortunate enough to join him along the way.

Sam Chaltain
Washington DC
Summer 2017

PREFACE

We left the Holiday Inn Express at about 6:30 a.m. after a brief huddle over powdered eggs and toast, just outside of Kansas City, Missouri. My fellow facilitators Charles Perry, Antwan Diggs, Johnny Hawkins, and I were going over our curriculum and plans for the two-day conference for the Kansas Department of Children and Families along with dozens of community service providers, church leaders, small nonprofits, and community advocates. It was our first day of training in the summer of 2015 with the Center for Neighborhood Enterprise, a Washington DC-based organization, which was founded by Mr. Robert Woodson, a brilliant civil rights leader, social activist, and advocate for community change and economic empowerment.

The Kansas City, Kansas, community was not different from others I had been in over the years: economically depressed, struggling for resources, and filled with passionate, intelligent, and dedicated people searching for solutions. We were driving west through Johnson County, Kansas, down Rainbow Boulevard, which bordered a more distressed Wyandotte County. The boundaries of these two disparate counties were the same as many across the country, a broad expanse of rail lines and an old steel bridge orange with eighty years of corrosion and decay, which separated these counties across racial and economic lines. We were driving toward a local community agency called the Avenue of Life, run by Desiree Monize, a passionate visionary and dedicated community leader and champion. Our summit for the next two days would take place in a small community space on the second floor of the newly renovated building that was home to the Avenue of Life.

The national philosophy of the Center for Neighborhood Enterprise we were sharing with the State of Kansas was not supplying answers but providing tools, resources, and suggestions to encourage dialogue and inspire collaborative strategies for local communities to find their own solution to the complex problems of child poverty, crime, drug and alcohol abuse, unemployment, and homelessness. After many years of work around the country, CNE had realized that local communities could be fortified with tools, resources, and technical assistance to develop local strategies for community empowerment.

Most communities contain the answers to many of their own challenges. It is only from within each community and through those who are closest to the problem can the real creative solutions be found. In his plenary speech on the first morning of our summit, Mr. Woodson shared the eloquent example of a ship coming into a harbor. How that ship's captain must relinquish control of his ship to the local harbormaster, who knows that port's sandbars and rocky shores as well as he knows himself. Woodson further explained that as a ship may come into port bringing goods and resources, only the local harbormaster can ensure their safe passage to the appropriate mooring.

How do we define who these leaders or harbormasters are in our communities? How do we communicate effectively and find collaborative solutions to common concerns? How can we support community leaders to leverage their growth experiences and share their stories of resiliency, renewal, and hope? These are some of the key questions we need to be asking in order to find sustainable solutions to our common community challenges. Though Woodson leans more to the conservative side and can often be seen with the likes of House Speaker Paul Ryan advising him on poverty initiatives, I have found his authenticity, directness, wisdom, and humility to be inspiring. He calls himself a "radical pragmatist." I think he would work with anyone, regardless of political ideology, who would help direct funds to the grassroots community leaders he so believes in.

In order to effectively address community challenges, there needs to be a deeper consciousness and purpose toward understanding our collective human condition. This understanding begins with the individual and our ability to bring our deeper morality, sense of justice, collaborative spirit, and belief in the ability of all people to grow, develop, and improve their circumstance, regardless of their position, status, and experience. In fact, many of our greatest leaders, advocates for social change, and community empowerment have come through their own life challenges. They have done the work of looking inward at their soul and have elevated themselves as role models, leaders, community capacity builders, and harbormasters. It is here within these individuals that our greatest example of purpose, consciousness, and growth orientation can be found. These people are the example of the building blocks to an individual and collective healing and opportunity for renewal and rebirth toward a cultural transformation in our country.

In this book, I differentiate our religious practices and traditions that give us comfort and strength, and, oftentimes, divide and separate us by dogma and focus on a universal spiritual presence that can unite us. It is our collective understanding of the soul that can provide insight and opportunity. I hope to explore the connection to our spiritual selves and an understanding of our soul purposefulness while we work on creating impact and connections in our communities. There is a great need for an individual and collective introspective journey discovering who we are, who we are meant to become as human beings, and how we can harness a deeper connection and shared consciousness.

I believe many of us have been led astray from our true spiritual path. Over time, we have allowed an imbalance and a faltering of human growth that has limited the development of our collective individual and spiritual potential. We need to recalibrate our sense of humanity, how to be thoughtful, empathetic, and compassionate. If we are to find connections and solutions, we must relearn and understand a new truer, more meaningful way of being, interacting, and communicating with one another.

The following chapters contain conversations between community leaders and change agents from around the country who have agreed to share their personal and professional stories. I have shared some of my own reflections and experiences as well as anecdotes and stories over twenty years as a social worker, change agent, and community advocate. The individuals highlighted in this book are friends and colleagues, with whom I have worked with and/or traveled across the country on various projects and community building efforts. The framework for each of their stories is guided by the same set of questions, but the interview has allowed for variation in discussion and open conversation. Not only are these individuals an incredible collection of community leaders, educators, and change agents from across the country; but more importantly, they are talented, passionate, beautiful human beings. All of them have agreed to share their insights, reflections, faith, spiritual beliefs, challenges, opportunities, and hope for the future. My desire is to provide optimism in the greatness that is our collective human spirit to overcome common community challenges, to be innovative, to harness our spiritual strength, and to find ways to understand a deeper soul consciousness.

CHAPTER 1

Roberto Carlos Rivera

Chicago, Illinois

Contrary to what we may have been taught to think, unnecessary and unchosen suffering wounds us but need not scar us for life. It does mark us. What we allow the mark of our suffering to become is in our own hands.

—bell hooks

Roberto Rivera and I met in 2011 while I was working as the executive director of the McCormick Tribune YMCA in Logan Square with the YMCA of Metropolitan Chicago. He was presenting a new curriculum he had developed called Fulfill the Dream, which engaged at-risk youth through the language and art of hip-hop culture. He explained how the blues, gospel, and jazz traditions that inspired hip-hop in the late 1970s were perfect access points for youth to find self-expression through art, dance, spoken word, and music and to capture their unique voice. I knew immediately this would be a positive path for our youth in the Teen REACH program to find connection, an outlet for expression, and mentorship. As we began talking over the next weeks and months, we realized that we shared a mentor from the University of Wisconsin at Madison: Professor Craig Werner. Even though we met him almost fifteen years apart from each other, he had a similar influence. Craig Werner was not only a brilliant professor but also someone who helped to guide and inspire both Roberto and me. Even though we came from different backgrounds, we had found a calling in the field of youth development and community empowerment. Needless to say, Roberto and I connected immediately and became friends in the common work and mission we shared. The following interview took place on a warm summer evening in my backyard, over a few especially cold Heinekens.

Stephen: Tell me about who you are, where you come from, and the work you do in the community.

Roberto: So my name is Roberto Carlos Rivera. My father is Nicaraguan, and my mother is American. My father was a baseball maniac. His name for himself was "CBM," the "Crazy Baseball Maniac." So I am actually named after Roberto Clemente. My entire upbringing, man, was centered around playing baseball.

Stephen: Do you still play?

Roberto: So my whole life was planned out for me. My pops had me playing little league. He lied about my age, so I never played T-ball.

Stephen: Where was this, in Chicago?

Roberto: I was born in Madison, Wisconsin, and my family moved to Texas when I was ten. I always played with older kids. He wanted me to, you know, not be intimidated. So playing baseball was a big part of my upbringing. I remember having the realization, you know. He said, "You're gonna play for the Nicaraguan national team every summer. You'll go to this college and play for this team because they went to the world series, and then by that time, you'll get into triple A baseball."

Stephen: Wow, he really had plans. Do you still have family in Nicaragua?

Roberto: Yeah, my father is still down there. So you know, I feel like the whole baseball piece was a big part of my life. I told my dad, "You know, I love you, but this is not my dream. It's your dream."

Stephen: That's tough. How old were you when you said that?

Roberto: I was eighteen, man.

Stephen: You were at least old enough to have a sense of self.

Roberto: Yeah, eighteen, I had just tried out with the Kansas City Royals.

Stephen: Oh shit, so you were a real baller! You tried out with the Royals?

Roberto: I was a serious player, and I just felt like there was so much pressure on me from my dad. I realized this is not what I wanted to do.

Stephen: Wow, this must have been a real pivotal point in your life.

Roberto: It was. I remember exactly where we were. I told my dad, "This is your dream, not mine. I'm not going to play baseball." The look on his face, he was heartbroken. To be honest, from that point, it felt like we never had the same energy or dynamic.

Stephen: Until now?

Roberto: So I mean the relationship with my dad is complex. My brother was born late in life. He had Down syndrome and autism. He was one of those presences in my life. I really learned a lot from him and from my grandfather. So getting back to the question of who I am and where I'm from, I spent most of my time in Madison, Wisconsin, and Galveston, Texas. You know, my father had a lot of problems. Once I counted up the number of schools I went to before high school . . . it was thirteen.

Stephen: Because you guys moved, or your dad pulled you?

Roberto: We would flee, man. My dad would get into stuff that I really don't want to get into detail about. So we would leave in the middle of the night and, you know, stay with family and friends. I went to school in Colorado. I lived in Miami. I lived in California and La Crosse, Wisconsin. Just all over the place, a bunch of random spots. So people ask, "Where are you from?" I would say, "Man, I'm from everywhere." You know, that would be my answer. I wasn't trying to be a smart-ass or anything. He finally kicked some of his bad habits when I was ten but then became a workaholic and disappeared six months out of the year. For me, that positive role model was my grandfather. So when my mother and father split, my mother said she was moving back to Madison and asked if I would go with her. What she didn't know was that was the time I told my father I wasn't playing baseball anymore. I was looking for a job and couldn't find one, so I started hustling. I was selling weed. I had a sense that there was a purpose that was bigger, but I just couldn't find it. I had no idea how to get there.

I remember coming home one night, high and drunk and looking in the mirror, and I didn't recognize myself. I remember crying out to God, "Man, God, if you're there, I just need help. I just can't figure this out and escape on my own." So when my mom said she was moving to Madison, my dad had been crazy and made some threats, some crazy stuff. So I moved to Madison with my mom in 1996. They say, "You can take people out of Egypt, but you can't take Egypt out of the people." So I came up to Madison with a quarter pound of weed and manifested the same reality as in Texas.

Stephen: I'm sure you found a lot of pot-smoking college students.

Roberto: All my friends became dealers there, but my grandfather, man, I call him my Michelangelo. He was the one who could see the sculpture trapped in the statue. He was like, "You should go back to school, go to college." He would introduce me to people like I was someone important.

Stephen: Was he also from Madison?

Roberto: Yes, Madison. He was a professional there, a community dude. He would introduce me to his peers, like, "This is my grandson Roberto." He was proud of me. I was like, "Why are you introducing me to these people? I'm nobody."

Stephen: He believed in you.

Roberto: I was just a guy who had a lot of pain. So it wasn't until . . . Man, serendipitously, he passed seventeen years ago yesterday. That funeral was a turning point in my life. I got to see the full fruit of his legacy and being a community worker and all the lives he had touched, the folks he had mentored and served on boards with and impacted people's lives in a profound way. When I saw this legacy of his community work and I understood he had pain in his life as well, I realized he saw my potential but also saw my pain. He believed I could one day take my pain and use it as propane—to transform my life and transform the world. That was the day, seventeen years ago yesterday, that I said I'm done.

Stephen: How old are you now?

Roberto: I said, "I'm done hustling . . . I'm done doing all this shit." I want to be positive and leave a legacy. So I'm thirty-six now. I was nineteen then.

Stephen: That's really a critical point in your life . . . With that in mind, I have a question: You said that before you left for Madison, you spoke to God. At age eighteen, how did you have a relationship with God? Did you always have that relationship? Where did you get the connection to have such an impactful and meaningful dialogue with a higher power?

Roberto: I remember going to church when I was about ten, mainly because my dad was getting sober and going to AA. He was brought up as a Catholic, and we would go to the Catholic church. I remember being excited to finish church and get breakfast or donuts. I wasn't much interested in what happened inside church. Once he got sober, he leaned more to focusing on work, and we moved to Texas. He was a mechanic and fixed cars, brought them to Latin America, and sold them for a profit. The profession he chose took him out of the country for much of the time. From age twelve to eighteen, I only saw my father six months out of the year. He would come back with different ideas. He came back from his travels with different ideas. He became a Muslim, and there was a big conflict with my mother who was born Southern Baptist, which created a challenge. They both wanted me to convert to their religion, and there was a sort of tug-of-war with my parents. I remember feeling that I really didn't want to follow either one.

On one of his trips, he came back talking about experiences with witchcraft, black magic, fortune telling, and really created a conflict with my mother's Christian background. During this time, my mother was pregnant with my brother, and she found out he had Down syndrome. The Creator hooked her up with some women that had tremendous faith. My father and mother had split, and my mom kept asking me to go to a prayer meeting with her. She didn't know I was hustling and selling drugs at the time. This was the last thing I wanted to go to. She asked me to go to a service at the home of one of her church sisters for a dedication for my brother. I said I would go, and I showed up reluctantly. There was actually a party that night that I was trying to get to. I told my friends I had something to do and would meet them later. Of course, I didn't tell them I was going to a prayer meeting with my mother. There were some older folks there, very friendly people, who were sharing testimonies. One older woman offered me cake and started to share a story with me. She began to go into this lengthy story about how God had told her to get in her car one night, and she started driving. She went a good distance and down a dirt road and forested area. The road opened and came to a clearing, and she saw a bunch of cars. When she turned on her brights, everyone began to scatter. When she drove closer, she saw that there was a black man being held by a bunch of Ku Klux Klan members about to hang him; and her lights had scared them away, thinking it was the police. She said that God had sent her to save this man's life that night.

Stephen: Was this in Wisconsin?

Roberto: No, this was Texas before I moved North. The group began praying for my brother, and the women turned to me and asked if I had ever been saved. I had told her that I had been to a Baptist school, but I'm not sure if I have actually been saved. She asked, "Have you been baptized in the Spirit?" She placed some oil on my head and began praying. She began speaking in another language or speaking in tongues. Then this little old lady blew on me. I was knocked to the ground. I felt like I was hit with a bolt of lightning. I had all this energy surging through my body, vroom . . . vroom . . . vroom. I felt a high that I never felt before. I felt a peace I never felt before. After some time had passed, I was laying on the ground and finally got up. She said, "Honey, you were just touched by God."

Stephen: Did you feel like you were touched by God?

Roberto: Yes, I did.

Stephen: Was that a turning point in your life?

Roberto: At that point, I didn't go to the party. I went home. Threw away all my cigarettes. Threw away all my dad's witchcraft books. I felt like I really knew that God was real. For a few days and weeks, I was preaching to my friends, even though I knew nothing about Scripture. I was telling them how God was real, but I didn't have any structure, and my friends really didn't get where I was coming from. After a few months, I began smoking again, but I needed another level of being high. It was at this point where I saw myself in the mirror that night and prayed to God. I left for Madison, Wisconsin, a few weeks later.

Stephen: So with all that history . . . I know you went back to school, got yourself on track, and began doing all this amazing work in your community. How have all these experiences fortified you? How does it all connect?

Roberto: What I realized is, like this older woman, that people can have a relationship with the Creator. She could dialogue and communicate. What I have come to find out through my spiritual journey is that God had a plan in my life to do something great. He wasn't going to just put me on the path and leave me alone but that I could check in and get insight and get direction. I would say that my grandfather's death was when I got off the track of destruction, but it wasn't until my brother died that I got off the track of distraction.

Stephen: When did your brother die?

Roberto: My brother died in 2005. So I created my own major at the University of Wisconsin. I was working, making some money. I bought my first house. My parents had never bought a house or had money. I was traveling, but when my brother died, I had a sense that this life, this good life, was not just about me making money but trying to make an impact.

I remember talking to my wife and telling her I wanted to make a deeper impact in the world. She helped me to write a business plan for our company.

Stephen: Was this the beginning of what is now the Good Life Organization?

Roberto: This was the first iteration called the Elements of Change based in Madison. I had a staff of five people and a business partner who helped us get it off the ground. I remember going to my brother's grave. I knew I was supposed to do stuff in schools, but I really didn't have a background in education. I remember praying at his grave, trying to figure out how I can connect with youth and make an impact. I got another one of those flashes from God at the grave site of my brother. It really transcends understanding. I started getting visions such as words flashing in front of me. I wrote them all down and started marinating on them. It went from bones to flesh to skin to a full curriculum.

We began implementing it in schools in Madison.

Stephen: So this was the development of your Fulfill the Dream curriculum?

Roberto: Yes, so we started impacting kids' lives. I feel like I have been cocreating this curriculum with the Creator. Even today, when I get invited to speak at a conference in front of a thousand people . . . the days leading up to it, I speak to the Creator and ask, "What do you want me to say?" I get moments of inspiration, and I write it all down. I do that with all my speeches.

Stephen: Tell me a little about the Good Life Organization. What do you guys do? Where has it manifested? How's it developing over time?

Roberto: Well, I was getting ready to start my masters in Afro-American studies in Madison when my wife was offered a job in Chicago. I ended up moving to Chicago with my wife. It was really in a strange place. My wife was working, and I was in a cocoon of sorts. I started writing lyrics and wrote an entire hip-hop album. I didn't know anyone in Chicago, so I kept to myself and asked God why he brought me to a city of millions to be by myself. The album that I wrote was called *First Fruits*. After a season of time, I started getting opportunities to go to LA and speak at a conference and connect with a community out there. They had asked me if I had a curriculum of material I could bring to their community. I said, "Sure I could." I had given up the old curriculum, but the same words and ideas were there, and that's how we began Fulfill the Dream. We worked with parents and youth, getting them to be the drivers of change in the communities. We unified all the organizations and rallied the executive directors and brought everyone together. We brought gang leaders out and started talking about a gang peace treaty. They opened up the avenues to allow youth to come to the program free of gang borders and territory. They started having conversations, and then every month, they began doing something called I Heart Wilmington, which was an activity and community gathering they did every month. This was the whole community getting together and being unified. It was a game shifter. So that was our first pilot of Fulfill the Dream. We came out after that with guns blazing. We did programmatic work in Chicago, Providence, Cincinnati, Madison, Milwaukee, and Beloit. Now we are doing work in Dallas, Texas. I just did my first training in Spain and recently got invited to present a TEDx talk.

Stephen: How does it feel to . . . be on a very successful path? You do a lot of amazing and powerful work. As you shared, you came from a place of your own destruction. Now you obviously have had a lot of success. What is that like?

Roberto: Well, I've come to develop my own philosophy on life and the meaning of life. That is that part of our purpose individually but also collectively—to take everything that we have, all our strengths, everything good that has happened in our lives, and also everything bad that has ever happened, and take that bundle and use that to serve our community, our city, our world. That is the purpose of life, I believe that. I'm at a point in my life where I have reflected on the things I have done and still cringe at. I think about the kids I got addicted to dope, smoking weed, and many of them are still on that path of destruction.

Stephen: Is it hard to acknowledge you played a role in that?

Roberto: All that stuff that has happened. I used to rob people, deal drugs, crazy stuff. I realized as terrible as all that stuff was, it gave me insight and an ability to relate in a way now that I couldn't otherwise. I am grateful for all of that, all the struggle. I ran away from home when I was thirteen, literally feeling helpless and hopeless. I tried to kill myself. In the Bible, Paul talks about it in the Scriptures. He says, "All my weaknesses and things I was ashamed of I am now boasting. God has used these things for good." Coming more from the Christian faith tradition, I believe everyone has a scripture written over their life. One of those scriptures over my life is Romans 8:28, which is, "God can use all things for a greater good for those who love him and are called according to his purpose." All the mess, all the knuckleheaded decisions that I have made have helped to create insight into reaching these kids. When we work with kids at Clemente High School in Chicago, for example, CPS officials will say, "Here are all the worst kids in the district." They have me do a keynote, but I see them not how they see them. I see them and their potential much in the same way my grandfather saw me.

Stephen: The Michelangelo vision?

Roberto: The Michelangelo vision.

Stephen: We have talked about a lot of your connection to spirituality and religion and you being touched by God. What do you believe the soul to be? How would you describe it?

Roberto: That's interesting because we talk about this in the curriculum. In terms that don't weird people out and allow us to go there in the public schools at this level. We have come to believe that human beings are multidimensional. We have a mind, body, heart, and soul. With those different domains and dimensions, we have different needs—that the mind has a need to learn, and the heart has a need to love. Just like plants need oxygen, sunlight, and water. Human beings are designed to be in a relationship to love. We need that. If youth don't get that when they're kids, they won't develop into empathetic human beings. Our body needs food, clothing, and shelter, and then there is the dimension of the soul that has a need to leave a legacy. We see folks in Chicago, in high-rise buildings making six and seven figures, doing all these things and being apparently successful at every level, but they are the ones most likely to commit suicide because there is a void in their life. They are neglecting the domain of the soul. Mother Teresa spoke on this when she first came to the United States. She saw the United States and was asked what she thought of our country, and she said, "This is the poorest country she has ever been to." She was obviously not referring to material poverty but spiritual poverty. So I think the soul is the part of us that hungers for purpose, that hungers for something larger than ourselves. I truly believe that all we do now will echo in all eternity, whether for good or for bad. Different people have different ideas of Heaven and Hell and so forth, but if you are putting out a bunch of negative energy in the world, your energy is going to be attracted to that when you leave the tent of the body. If you are doing good and bringing light, liberation, healing, and love . . . the source of that is where you belong. I think the soul is a part of who we are as individuals, but there is a soul of communities and soul of a city. I think the soul in many ways is like—if I were to use a metaphor—a jigsaw puzzle. My purpose in life is not fully fulfilled all by myself, but it's fulfilled in relationship and in community with other people that have that intentionality. That if we are all living this way, these jigsaw puzzle pieces start to come together and start to paint a picture of redemption for the world. It's an interdependent component.

Stephen: I hear what you are saying, but right now, for example, Chicago has the label "Chiraq." It's the hotspot, the most violent city in the country. Just this weekend, there were seventeen homicides. How do we start to make change? Talk is cheap. How do we start to work together with all these different organizations and community partners and find that purposefulness to actually make substantive change?

Roberto: That's the million-dollar question. I feel like it's important for people to regain their history. When they reclaim their history, they have the ability to make history. I think that folks need to understand that their story has value. An example is when we look at the phenomenon of post-traumatic growth.

Stephen: Can you explain that? A lot of people have heard of post-traumatic stress, but what is post-traumatic growth?

Roberto: Folks are familiar with post-traumatic stress disorder, you know, when people have been traumatized and that trauma is having a major effect on the psychological, physical, emotional, and cognitive components as a human being. So resiliency is when someone is going through trauma, and they are able to bounce back to the place where they were prior to that trauma taking place. Post-traumatic growth is a process where you are able to not only bounce back but also actually grow from the trauma you have experienced in your life. When different researchers look at this, it oftentimes happens most where these narratives of redemption and growth are being told to folks, where the community has passion, and individuals can begin telling their story with a support system and an expectation toward a growth orientation.

Getting back to Chicago . . . the storytelling we most often hear is stripped from the blues, jazz, and gospel impulses. In hip-hop, for example, the stories that are played on the radio now are not the redemptive stories that they used to be. The music that was very rich and had the DNA of a redemptive blues or gospel story is no longer being told. Urban youth that are dealing with a lot of trauma are in need of these redemptive traditions in order to find hope, resiliency, and voice. One of the steps toward becoming a post-traumatic growth community—and I believe this is a real purpose for Chicago—is to rise from the fires, ashes, and the violence we see now. The hope is for our youth to find that voice and regain that ability to tell new stories and author new narratives for their communities.

Stephen: You are in the front lines of the fire. You are working with the kids and young adults that have been locked up, have been shooting and dealing. That have been really at the core of the struggle here. What keeps you sustained and positive? You talk about PTSD. When you are around a lot of violence and negativity, you get secondary effects of trauma. What keeps you optimistic, hopeful, passionate, and resilient in your work?

Roberto: I think that part of our work with this population is that we have that Michelangelo vision of who they are. Society says they are at risk. Society says they are a problem. Society says they are broken. We see they are able to take positive risk, to be part of the solution. To not just be part of the change but agents of change. As we work with them in a way that allows them to serve their community to create their own businesses, to do something real and learn who they and one another are in the process. In many ways, to relate that to the spiritual piece, they are doing the work of the Kingdom. They are coming to experience their higher self and starting to live up to their higher self. What is amazing to me, being a facilitator in this process, is that it is a reciprocally transformative experience. When these young people step into their purpose and connect with their soul and regain authorship of their lives, schools, and communities, they experience that healing, and it is empowering for all of us. A lot of our inspiration, hope, and resiliency comes from the youth that we serve. When we can cocreate with folks, with peers, with youth, that is the essence of life. That's being part of something that is much greater than any individual. It's having a collective spiritual experience. It requires we do some work of our own, but that work is not for the edification of ourselves. It's for the edification of one another and for the community. It's a greater service to help bring up others. That's the real come up. Not just elevating ourselves but also that we are all uplifted in the process.

CHAPTER 2

Does the Soul Contain Melanin?

*What lies behind us and what lies before us are tiny
matters compared to what lies within us.*
—Ralph Waldo Emerson

I grew up in the Northside suburbs of Chicago. Evanston and Skokie, the two towns that bordered Chicago to the North and Northwest were a very interesting example of extremes. As in my example with the railroad tracks in Wyandotte County, Kansas, Evanston was sharply divided by the northern branch of the Chicago River and other distinct geographic boundaries. Though many of us growing up in Evanston did not succumb to the adult and older generational segregation that existed, it was nonetheless present and obvious as a part of the culture of the city. I would walk or ride my bike to high school almost every day across the north branch of the Chicago River into what is the fifth ward, where the local high school stood. Almost four thousand students from every walk of life went to Evanston Township High School. For some reason, which was never publicly discussed by most adults, the fifth ward was predominantly an isolated black neighborhood, struggling economically from many of the more affluent white and mixed neighborhoods of Evanston. One of the most ironic and obvious aspects of Evanston's disparity is the two-minute drive down Emerson Avenue, between the fifth ward and Northwestern University's campus, one of the country's most prestigious and wealthy institutions, situated on Evanston's lakeshore. The fifth ward is filled with many harbormasters, community leaders, as well as passionate, intelligent, and thoughtful people. Unfortunately, like many cities around the country, it is also plagued with pockets of poverty, high crime, gang violence, and other common challenges that we see across the urban landscape. As Evanston borders Chicago's Rogers Park neighborhood to the north, there is also a high-crime and high-violence corridor that is often in the news. Many local leaders in Evanston have struggled to find long-term sustainable answers to the challenges of economic and educational disparity, high unemployment, crime, and other social barriers that currently exist. Organizations such as the YWCA, Youth Options United, Family Focus, Infant Welfare Society of Evanston, the Moran Center, and many others have done excellent work in the areas of child care, youth development, early education, health disparity, legal advocacy, and teen programming. The faith-based community has also played a major role in the development of community empowerment efforts across economic, cultural, and social lines. However, many of the same issues and challenges still remain years after I left Evanston in the late 1980s. In fact, it was recently reported by the local school district that close to two hundred freshmen entered the 2017 school year at Evanston Township High School reading at a sixth-grade level. The majority of these students are from lower-income black and brown neighborhoods of Evanston. The educational and economic disparity that exists is very real.

My neighborhood was just across this river and bordered Skokie, which is a community known for its large Jewish and immigrant population as well as a somewhat more humble housing stock and lower cost of living. Skokie also contains a large Eastern European, Latino, Asian, and Muslim/Arabic population and has become an incredibly diverse and vibrant community. While Evanston has grown more diverse since my childhood, gaining significant Latino population in the fifth ward and Asian population in the Western, Southern, and Southwestern neighborhoods bordering Chicago, it is still plagued by sharp ethnic/racial and economic borders and huge disparity gaps. Since the 1980s, the Latino population has grown from 1 percent to 17 percent in Evanston, while the black population has reduced slightly to approximately 23 percent.

The specific Irish Catholic neighborhood that I grew up in was anchored by St. Joan of Arc, a beautiful Irish Catholic school and church three blocks from my home. This suburban landscape was different from the fifth ward down the street and across the river. It was exemplified by beautiful large old homes with double lots and multiple cars in the driveways. As the first Jewish family in this non-Jewish neighborhood of privilege in the early 1970s, it was very evident that some of the neighbors were not very pleased to see us move in. Like many growing up in our cities and towns where economic, racial, and ethnic lines crossed, intolerance, anti-Semitism, and bigotry would appear.

As a nonreligious Jew, not having been raised in a temple, my Jewishness was not really understood or known to me at a young age. It was my grandparent's Chanukah parties, my mother's few Yiddish words, matzah ball soup, occasional relatives' bar/bat mitzvahs, and my father's obsession with Stalin, Adolf Hitler, Nazi Germany, and the Holocaust that gave me an informal connection to my Jewish heritage. I would often hear stories from my father of how I too, had I lived in WWII Europe, would have been thrown into a boxcar, the gas chamber, and ultimately burned in an oven at Auschwitz or Sobibor. It would be much later in my life that I would want to explore more of my cultural and religious background.

When we first moved into our home in 1970, some had heard of their new Jewish neighbors and were not happy about it. There were some who, as kids unfortunately do, found ways to use hateful words such as "Kike," "Go home, Jew," and other slang terms that made little sense to me. I have a very strong memory of being intimidated and chased by older boys in the neighborhood. One day, while playing on a swing set in Central Park, a few blocks from my house and local elementary school, I heard someone above me standing on the bathroom structure screaming "Go home Jew!" and throwing asphalt roof tiles toward my direction, one hitting me in the back as I turned away. I ran home crying and told my fourteen-year-old elder brother, who, without hesitation, ran back to the park and proceeded to smash this boy's Schwinn ten speed to pieces. This was one of many encounters. A few years later, another Jewish family down the block unfortunately had swastikas and the words "Hitler" and "Nazi" scrolled onto the side of their home in black paint. Not surprisingly, this young family moved from the neighborhood rather quickly.

It was in these fights and defenses of my identity that I began to feel my "otherness." I realized I was different from other white people in my neighborhood. Although my white skin and families' economic status provided the same privilege and opportunities as other white people in this community, there was something curious and different about my identity that I struggled to understand. How did ten-year old children learn to use anti-Semitic language and participate in hate crimes and violence against others?

This same attitude and prejudicial behavior was echoed by many "good-intentioned" white people toward black folks in Evanston. It was cultural ignorance, privilege, and fear of difference that was most apparent to me. There were occasional overt racial issues and discriminatory acts in the local news, but mostly, it was unspoken and quiet. When many white folks crossed the river on their drive downtown for dinner, I would not be surprised if they pretended not to notice the neighborhood changes and simply roll up their windows and lock their doors out of fear. The windows would come down again once they got to Ridge Avenue, another line of racial and economic demarcation. At the same time, there were some white residents in Evanston that were more conscious and "woke" and worked alongside black and brown folks on the side of justice and equity and truly had the right motivations for fighting against the issues that plagued the city and indeed much of the rest of our country.

Another one of the more distinct memories I have of overt racism and anti-Semitism in Evanston was in seventh grade. My close group of male friends consisted of seven of us—a typical pack of twelve-year-old pre-teen boys. One Monday afternoon, we found out there was a dance being put on by some group of Evanston elites that was apparently the thing to do if you were in seventh grade in the early '80s. Later in the week, one by one, my friends started talking about the dance and the formal invitation they had received. Of course, there were also discussions of who would invite who for a date and what the plans for the night would be. As the days passed, I started wondering why I hadn't gotten an invitation. That Friday, I remember standing in a circle with my two non-white friends from our group in front of Haven Middle School just staring at one another thinking why we hadn't gotten the invitation. Almost simultaneously, we understood . . . and became very quiet. Our hearts sank. I felt the blood rush to my face, swallowed hard and wanted to swear and curse and tell these people what I thought of them. It was hard not to take it personally. In fact, it was distinctly personal. We were quiet for a few long seconds. The Jewish, black, and Filipino kids in our group were not welcome. It was us. We were not invited . . . We were not welcome. It was me. Everyone else in our circle of friends was white and Christian. It was the only answer that made sense. We were exactly correct. Somehow it was an accepted practice that this private group of upper-class, privileged Evanston folk only invited white, Christian people to their seventh-grade event. My understanding is that to this day, thirty-five years later, this party exists, and black, brown, and other groups have made their own balls and events as a counter to this carry-over of elitism, institutionalized racism, prejudice, and bigotry. How

17

does a twelve-year-old process all those emotions and feelings of rejection and "otherness"? You don't, really. You just keep on moving, knowing that you are not really accepted or wanted by the larger culture of the town you have grown up in. Then you write about it thirty-five years later in a chapter of your book discussing racism, anti-Semitism, and prejudice.

Keep in mind Evanston was like many integrated communities in the '70s and '80s in the United States. We were struggling to make sense of emerging from a world of racial segregation, even in the North; integrating schools with busing, combining the white and black YMCA, and existing in shared spaces: community centers, restaurants, and places of worship. Of course, black kids were the ones bused out of their community into white communities, and the Y that was shut down was the black one. While Evanston is seen, and many would argue, to be a progressive and forward-thinking community, there were and still are deep veins of racism and prejudice as in many places across the country. It was and is supported and fueled by our geographic and economic isolation and segregation. Some neighborhoods have taken a long time to change, along with people's hearts and minds. Some hearts and minds have never changed. It is here, within our heart, where our ignorance and fear of other resides and is most pronounced and, unfortunately, often ignored.

With that being said, many of my generation as well as others before and after came out of Evanston with a strong sense of valuing inclusion and strength from the diversity that existed. I have many memories of an early awareness of the diversity and opportunity to engage others that was layered into this complex community. I recall having conversations with my teenage friends about issues of race, class, segregated communities, and how we all fit or did not fit into the culture of our city. We always felt that, compared to other communities, our diversity and efforts toward inclusion, though not always successful, made us special. I often reflect on my upbringing in Evanston, and I am thankful for all I was able to experience, both the positive and the negative. It has had much to do in shaping who I am today and the choices I have made in my life. I am very thankful for that.

On our drive to the Avenue of Life one morning in Kansas City, one of my colleagues was discussing an exchange between two of our conference participants regarding religion and faith the previous day. One, a devout Christian and believer in the Word, was sharing her opinion of Christianity and faith in relation to our community challenges in a large group discussion. All of a sudden, the words "ISIS" and "nonbelievers" were heard, and voices began getting very loud. The other responded in a sharp and elevated tone, "I was raped by so-called Christians." The facilitators quickly pulled the group back from the brink of a verbal altercation. As we reflected in our car ride the next day, the question, which rolled so loosely out of my colleagues' mouth, was asked: "Is there racism in Heaven?" We all laughed somewhat uncomfortably. I thought that this was such an interesting question. "Of course not," we all said after a few seconds. This was an interesting thought. Heaven and God transcend our earthly human prejudices, ignorance, and failings, don't they?

I think of the first time I actually saw a black Jesus hanging on the wall in a home. It was in the house of one of my friends from my case manager days in Chicago. I was in my early twenties. We had finished a case manager training at the South Side Chicago Department of Children and Family Services (DCFS) office on a Friday afternoon on Sixty-Third and Ashland. My colleague and friend Walter invited me to hang out at his apartment, which was only ten minutes away. I walked into the expansive four-story 1930s yellow brick South Side multiunit building. My eyes followed the long oak hardwood floors back to the kitchen. It was there that I noticed the painting of Jesus on the wall. The discussion of the Bible followed and a quote shared from Revelations chapter 1: "He had hair of wool and feet of bronze." This was the first time I was exposed to this knowledge, and it had seemed the earth had shifted that day. I think it might have also been the first time my friend had invited a white Jewish person to his home. In my young naïve mind, every image, church painting, television ad, and Sunday school flyer I had seen all had Jesus portrayed as white, with flowing brown hair and blue eyes. The idea of a black or bronze Jesus hanging from white pulpits across America just doesn't seem to be a realistic option, but why? Is it not a valid quote from the Bible? How do we, as a nation, begin to move beyond our struggle with race, ethnicity, and identity?

In the early '90s, I worked for an old settlement house in Chicago's Northwest Side neighborhood. It was founded in the turn of the century by a colleague of Jane Addams, one of the founders of the modern social work movement. I was hired as a bilingual case manager in my early twenties, working with predominantly Latino children who were wards of the State of Illinois in the Department of Children and Family Services of Chicago. We helped to place children in foster care or homes of relatives if possible. We provided services, support, and advocated for these children in the juvenile justice system. Many times, our efforts focused on rehabilitation and supportive services for the parents of these children and helping them navigate through the language and cultural barriers that existed between the State of Illinois and the Latino community. We worked toward a place in their case management services that would allow for reunification with their family if possible.

When unification was not an option due to drug use, abusive behavior, or simply a lack of interest, we would try to find adoptive parents for our children. We would start by looking for relatives, but if a relative was not found, we would look for a traditional placement and, ultimately, an adoptive home. This adoption process could take months, as we wanted to ensure a strong and stable bond was achieved, that prospective parents and our foster children could develop a relationship and a successful transition to finding a stable home. On one of these visits, I accompanied a fellow case manager to the South Side home of an adoptive family. This adoptive family had already participated in multiple visits with a beautiful young girl who had been abandoned by her mother at an early age and had no relatives capable of taking her in. This was her sixth and a culminating visit as a precursor to the process of adoption and a permanent home for this intelligent little girl. As I waited in front of the home in the car, my colleague and her client went inside for their final adoptive visit. When they returned to the car about an hour later, I could tell that something had not gone well. I could see it in my colleagues' facial expression. It was clear we could not discuss what transpired in front of an eight-year-old, hopeful that her "new parents" would start the process of adoption. I will never forget, later that day, after we dropped off our client at her foster home in Humboldt Park, what my colleague shared with me. We sat in the car in silence for some time, and then she began quietly. The adoptive African-American family had spent hours and multiple successful visits with this young girl. They had carefully considered an adoption to provide stability, safety, and the hope of a home and parents who would finally provide love and care to this beautiful little human being. The adoptive family had simply stated to my colleague that they would not be moving forward with the adoption process. Our client, this beautiful soul, had a complexion that was apparently too dark, too black for their family. They had said, "She simply did not fit in." Her skin color did not meet their imaginary color line, self-imposed by internalized racism and intra-cultural hatred. I thought, *How in the world would a black family not adopt a beautiful, intelligent girl simply because of the amount of melanin in her skin?* My understanding and insight into the complexity of prejudice, racism, and the color line forever changed that day.

I have been married for twenty years. My three children are Puerto Rican and Jewish. We affectionately have termed them as "Jew-Rican." I often think about their experience growing up biracial in the new millennium. I find it frustrating how our society has not figured out how to make simple changes to acknowledge people who don't fit in traditional racial and ethnic boxes such as the census or applications for employment. I think about the frustration and challenges growing up biracial in our society and how it must be confusing for many young people. However, at the same time, we are starting to see more interracial relationships on TV and in the media to the point where it is becoming an accepted identity, even trendy, at least in some communities and areas of the country. My wife and I have tried to surround our kids with a very diverse and open-minded community of family, friends, and loved ones. In fact, whether intentionally or by accident, many of our friends are in inter-racial relationships and have biracial children, and it seems to be the norm more than an anomaly. Now that my children are older, and we can begin to speak about these issues, I am fascinated by their openness and willingness to embrace the diversity in their world: whether race, class, gender, sexual orientation or belief system. However, it is often others, even extended family members, that find it difficult to classify them in the "correct" racial or ethnic box. I remember my oldest daughter sharing with me, on her first day of high school orientation at Lane Tech, one of the largest public schools in the city, someone asking her what she "was," referring to her ethnicity. She replied, "Jewish and Puerto Rican." The response from the girl who asked on that first day of high school was, "How does that work?"

I am not sure about the answer to the question, "Is there racism in Heaven?" The answer probably doesn't have much relevance for those of us struggling for equality, social justice, shared opportunity, and an inclusive culture in our communities and cities. It is clear to me, however, through these and other stories, that we have, for the most part, gotten much of it wrong here on earth.

CHAPTER 3

Loren Fardulis

San Diego, California

*God doesn't give us what we can handle, God
helps us handle what we are given.*

—Unknown

Loren and I met in the spring of 2003. He knew my wife, Marlene, and her family through their affiliation with the Seventh-day Adventist boarding school my wife attended in the early '80s. Loren was employed there as a counselor, teacher, and youth leader. We met one evening at a gathering of friends and family in Chicago and clicked immediately. Though Loren was twenty years my senior, we had very similar perspectives on youth development, the role mentoring played in the life of adolescents, and a belief in our ability to make impact in the lives of others. We very quickly began conversations about opportunities in the State of Illinois and potential work in residential treatment with the Department of Children and Family Services. Over the next few months, we embarked on a plan to develop a nonprofit company called Mosaic Youth Homes and Family Services. We worked on this strategy and business plan for over two years, making great progress. We even received an agreement from the Department of Children and Family Services to award us a contract upon securing site funding. Unfortunately, as with many new businesses, start-up capital proved to be a challenge. Loren is an inspiring leader, counselor, and administrator in youth development, family services, and residential treatment. His passion, leadership, and energy are infectious. He also has a deep spiritual grounding and belief in family and faith that is inspiring. We met for this interview on a beautiful weekend in the fall of 2016 in San Diego, California, where Loren lives with his wife, Paula.

Stephen: Tell me about yourself? Your background, where you came from, and what you do?

Loren: As I contemplate that question, I have to start with where I am. I consider myself a colored leaf in the cycle of human life. Where I came from as a boy growing up in the house of a great aunt who raised me from the age of three. My mother was present, but she had left my dad. She divorced him. I grew up as a kid with some pretty strong women in my life, especially my aunt. She was capable of running any Fortune 500 company. She was a wise, prudent woman who knew how to handle finances equal to her strength. I feel, looking back as a colored leaf, I like the idea that I had her as both a mother and a father figure. I came out of Miami, Florida, where there was a lot of diversity: racially, religiously, and culturally. We moved a lot. I don't even know the reasons why. Always had nice homes. Always had opportunity to be around a lot of diversity.

Stephen: When you say you moved a lot, was this all in Florida or just the Miami area?

Loren: Miami area.

Stephen: What was the time frame? How old were you?

Loren: Starting at the age of three and through the age of high school, I'm going to say about fourteen years.

Stephen: Was this the '50s or '60s?

Loren: Yes, '50s. [*Laughter*]

Stephen: Is that why you call yourself a colored leaf?

Loren: Yeah, when you are sixty-nine years old, you can call yourself whatever you want. As I look back, I feel really blessed. I had a great childhood even though I didn't have a father. It plagued me a bit. In that era, people who didn't have fathers were seen as odd. So I grew up with that stigma. I had a few fights about it, but overall, I had a great childhood—treated well and given a lot of wisdom from the women around me.

Stephen: Can I ask you about your father? Why did he leave?

Loren: Yeah, my father was a man with absolutely no values and integrity. He loved women and sex. Very unfaithful to my mother. In fact, he was engaged to be married to another woman when he married my mother. In fact, he married to both all at the same time. She divorced him. I never saw him again till I was thirty-six years old. Never saw him, never heard from him.

Stephen: Wow . . . that has to be a pretty powerful childhood trauma or reflection.

Loren: It was . . . During that time, I saw myself as the oddball out. The idea that I couldn't talk about a father. I wasn't the only kid, but it was uncommon during that time. Men were back from the war. To not have a father around created some real problems for me. You know . . . where was my male role model?

Stephen: Did you find a role model somewhere as a boy?

Loren: I was good with the support I had, but because my aunt really encouraged me in sports—I mean, really encouraged me—I became very good at baseball. Yes, that male support showed up as a college man who came to the YMCA. He took a bunch of us street rats and turned us into a baseball team. He was the difference in my life at that time. He came along at the right time. He saved me, I believe.

Stephen: I don't want to jump ahead too far, but that is an interesting reflection for your work, right—who you have become and who I know you to be.

Loren: Yes, one of the interesting things as I grew and became interested in girls, adolescent development, gender issues, dating, and that kind of thing. One thing that became profound for me and was a real issue was that I wanted to become a father and a damn good father. I wanted to be there for my children.

Stephen: As a reaction to your own experience.

Loren: Yeah, as a reaction to my dad not being there for me. It definitely had an impact on me.

Stephen: So in Miami . . . you talked about being a teenager. What was school like? Did you go to college? Did you start working? What did you do after those teenage years?

Loren: I grew up in a Christian family. My granddaddy and granny were Nazarene circuit preachers and—

Stephen: Circuit preachers? Help me out with that one.

Loren: Well, the guys who rolled up a tent down the road, had tent meetings, and had a circuit they preached in. They were preachers in the South and had a circuit they worked. My aunt influenced my life, definitely . . . from the standpoint of another strong women in my life. My mother was not a strong woman. She was rather sickly, and the courts were going to take us and put us in foster care. My aunt stepped up and kept us and the family together. It was her. My granny and my mom and I had my great aunt's husband, Uncle Harry . . . Boy, he was quite abusive physically.

Stephen: To you?

Loren: Oh yeah . . . and my two siblings. You know it was a situation where the only positive thing I learned from him was his work ethic. He worked hard and treated people fair regardless of who they were. Paid well. But, boy, he was the enemy. The primary thing with the abuse with us kids was the idea that we invaded his home. They had no children before us.

Stephen: This was your aunt's husband?

Loren: Yes. He did not welcome us. There was tension all throughout our time together through high school. My aunt made sure we went to Christian school. From there, I went to a Christian college, spitting, biting, and clawing the whole way. I didn't want to do it. I had my goals set on professional baseball, but I had that Christian background. A lot of values and great teachers. I can name four or five great teachers at each grade level. Great people. They affected my life. I got to a point where I recognized that being a coach and working with kids became a greater calling for me. Greater than playing baseball.

Stephen: It sounds like it also took that place or desire of wanting to be a father figure.

Loren: Absolutely. Absolutely. I had a great work ethic and got out of college with no debt. I had a couple of really good jobs and paid my whole way. When I finished, it meant a lot to me to have paid my own way through a private Christian education, but I still struggled . . . See I grew up as a child and a teenager always looking over my shoulder . . . to see if my uncle was there. He had this habit of slapping me in my right ear upside my head. So I developed this mind-set like am I good enough. He would send me to go get something in a drawer, and I would go in there and just get so tense about the outcome. Would I come back with the wrong thing and get hit?

Stephen: Like a trauma reaction.

Loren: Oh yeah, it was. That followed me through life. College in particular. Am I good enough? Can I really do it? That kind of thing.

Stephen: So your coaching, education, Christian background kind of led you into your career path?

Loren: It did. One more element around that was when I finished high school, I had the opportunity that summer before college started. I had the opportunity to be the coach at the same YMCA, where that coach saved my butt years ago. In Miami, there were rain storms that blew in and then blew out; and one day, I was in the right field cleaning up a mud puddle for the game we were going to have that night, and I had an epiphany. This epiphany or voice said, "Loren, you are getting ready to go through college. Go through it and relax because what you are meant to do is to take care of kids who are wards of the state.

Stephen: This is when you were eighteen? Was this a spiritual experience, a God-inspired thing? Did you really hear a voice, or it just popped in your head?

Loren: Well, I was thinking about my future, but it wasn't like I was really processing it. I believe "somebody" was telling me this outside of myself. I was a Christian. I did believe it was a spiritual thing or from God, but I had no idea back then what it really meant.

Stephen: Most eighteen-year-old kids don't have that kind of experience.

Loren: I went to college and got my degree in health, recreation, and physical education, a minor in mathematics and psychology. It really became a touching point to hear about and understand a bit about psychology. My career, starting off as a coach, what that taught me. The experience taught me about my own voice. Some of the knowledge and how to use it with kids and how to communicate. It was critical for me deciding to go for my master's degree. They wanted to pay for me, the school I was teaching at in Chicago.

Stephen: What school was that?

Loren: Broadview Academy, a Seventh-day Adventist boarding school in the Western Suburbs. I got my master's degree. They wanted me to go on an educational administrative track, but that voice inside me wouldn't let me do it. I knew it was a solid career, but I changed it to psychology. That's where my eyes were opened. It was about 1982 when I finished my degree.

Stephen: I know that you have a passion for working with youth. We've worked together in group homes and with severely troubled youth in the DCFS system. What got you from working in a school setting to working in residential treatment?

Loren: That's an interesting question. I specialized in behavioral modification. My eyes began to open up to therapy and counseling . . . the good it can do and how could I mesh this with the work I wanted to do with children. It brought me back to those words I heard when I was eighteen. Thinking back to those words about working wards of the state, at-risk kids, severely disturbed children.

Stephen: Okay . . . so I have to stop and ask you this question. To me, I believe that things just don't happen. When you had these "words" that you heard—and years later connecting to an experience that you had at eighteen—how do you define that? Was it God-inspired? Was it your destiny? What is your spiritual take on that? It seems it was pretty profound to have your entire career clarified to you in a mudhole in a baseball field when you were eighteen. How do you explain that?

Loren: I firmly believe that, yes . . . it was the source of life in me and talking to me and me talking to myself. I believe this thing we call God, I see as more of a spiritual dynamic. I am connected. All of us are connected to that source we call God. I believe it's that energy, that force. My mind was ready for it. The only way I know how to define it is Spirit.

Stephen: This book has a lot to do with spirituality and the building of community and making connections. How do you connect those dots with your spirituality and the work you do with vulnerable populations in the community?

Loren: I guess I might relate it to something like . . . all of us as human beings are looking for purpose. Some may start off in fields where they are focused on making money, but I can't tell you how many people have called me—lawyers, bankers, doctors—who say, "I want to do something different in my life. How can I get involved with what you are doing? I need meaning in my life." I really believe that all of us are looking for that purpose . . . that emerald city that creates meaning for us. One day, when I was a principal at a boarding academy in Oregon, I woke up at about one in the morning with all these thoughts racing in my mind . . . I couldn't keep up with it . . . It was this work we have been talking about. I told my wife I had to go and just drive. I went to a Denny's restaurant at two in the morning. I didn't leave till six in the morning, and when I left, I had a bunch of napkins I had written on. It was about working with wards of the state.

Stephen: So what did you write out?

Loren: The thing that came to me was working with these severely emotionally disturbed kids. I started writing about what type of program would you offer the court system, the human services system to transform these kids. That was the question I began to write to. I wrote out a full program I called the Monarch model.

Stephen: You mean like monarch butterfly?

Loren: Yeah. [*Loren shows left forearm tattoo of a monarch butterfly*] The issue at this point was really an outline of a full-program model. I sat and talked with my wife and showed her what I put together.

Stephen: Almost divinely inspired. Whatever language you put to it, it sounds inspired by a higher power?

Loren: I truly believe so. Within six weeks, I had resigned from the school in Oregon and was ready to start this program. It was the concept of the metamorphosis of the butterfly. I became well acquainted with how that translates into the needs and development of human beings. The progression of maturation.

Stephen: So this set you off on the path of running Monarch Youth Homes in California?

Loren: Yes.

Stephen: I have had multiple people in these interviews for this book share similar stories. It's not the first time I have heard of this type of profound moment. A moment that is almost inexplicable that provided clarity, insight, or profound information. I have to ask this question . . . I'm not quite sure how to frame this question. Do you believe, as we walk through our lives, is there a higher power not only present but also feeding us and guiding us to our life's purpose?

Loren: I believe that 100 percent. Nothing happens by accident, I believe that. It's a miraculous thing. There's a guiding force of life, and It's not only all powerful but also gives us freewill. What if I laid back down and said—I don't know—I was having a nightmare or whatever and didn't listen to myself. I think that as we walk through life, the more we allow ourselves to listen to our voice, the more we will hear it. In my humble opinion, it only has one thing in mind—that we live an abundant life. I don't mean just financially, not at all. I'm talking about living an abundant life, a fulfilled life. How can I do that if I am not in touch with my divine purpose? Why I am here. I believe people will know it when they feel it. I thought coaching was my divine purpose. I was damn good at it. I learned all sorts of skills with kids and parents, but it wasn't my divine purpose. It was developing from that experience at the age of eighteen when I had that vision in the baseball field all the way through my master's degree work to now. It's brighter now than it was. It makes sense. Our journey and other things come into play. One of the great pieces of my journey that reinforced me was the work you and I did together. It has made my purpose even more profound. It's divine intervention.

Stephen: Do you believe that . . . just like you said in your answer, "the more we listen to that voice." Do you believe that regardless of tradition, faith, culture, geography, position . . . that it is a human opportunity?

Obviously, we all live in different circumstance, some in severe poverty, extreme personal challenges . . . but do we all have that innate ability to connect with that voice?

Loren: I do because we are all human. I have personal experiences with those in poverty or extreme prejudices who have found that voice as well. I have heard enough and seen enough in my years to say yes, but circumstances happen. Things happen, but we are most often given another choice. One of the great questions in life is, are you going to get up off the mat? Where is your courage? Where is your strength, your belief system? Get up! But there is a lot of noise out there.

Stephen: Just from knowing you, there have been ups and downs, struggles and successes, the highs and lows of your own career working with young people. What are some things you have learned through your own life journey?

Loren: I think most people would like to have something they are known for. It's part of their self-worth. Most want to be givers, not just takers. What is it that propels us to listen to that voice? What is it that inspires us to get up when it would be easy to just be a victim and say, "I guess my dream wasn't that important anyway." I'll tell you a story. One of the things that I almost allowed to ruin my life was the death of my daughter. I can tell you firsthand that I wasn't a nice person to be around during that time. I didn't want to see anyone. Didn't want to talk . . . I just wanted everyone to just go to hell. I wanted God to not exist. I hated God.

Stephen: Could you tell me what happened to your daughter?

Loren: My daughter is the one who gave me the courage to step out from being a principal. Shortly after she visited me, I had that epiphany late at night where I wrote all that stuff down. She was studying to be a social worker. She wanted to join her poppa at Monarch Youth Homes. She was on her way back from Albuquerque, New Mexico, on her way to Farmington, and she was in a car accident. A lady was driving with three other kids in the back seat, and my daughter was in the passenger side. A bunch of deer jumped out in front of the car, and the driver oversteered. It flipped several times, and Amy was killed. She was the only one killed.

Stephen: Jesus . . .

Loren: In the process of that pain, my wife and people said, "Loren, how is healing going to ever take place?" So we went to the accident site, and in the process of doing that, to make a long story short, we saw this huge storm from the west coming from New Mexico. You know how the sky gets inky blue? The winds were blowing off the high desert. My son was driving, and I was in the back seat. Candidly, I was cursing God. I was full of anger. There were questions such as "Where were you, God?", "Was there something more important you were doing?", "Where were the angels for my daughter?" So I got really arrogant and just shouted out. It upset my son. I said, "If you are really out there, then paint her damn name right there in the sky so I can see it." I just demanded it. A few miles down the road, there was this cloud off to our left in the shape of an arm with a hand opened to the sky. Right above the hand were three clouds that spelled out her name: A-M-Y.

Stephen: Everybody saw the same thing? What did you guys do?

Loren: We stopped . . . pulled the car over.

Stephen: Just in awe?

Loren: In awe. The words that came to my mind were, "Loren, do you think I don't know who Blondie is?"—that was my nickname for her—"You don't have to worry. She is in my hands."

Stephen: Inexplicable.

Loren: Just inexplicable. So the issue is that all people are going to be challenged. Some are challenged right out of the womb. Some in high school. Some in college. Some later in life. Whatever. Most of us will be challenged many times with very important issues such as . . . where am I going to sleep? Where am I going to eat? Get clothes? How am I going to get money? I just really believe with all those challenges, we are also here for a purpose. If we are just willing to listen, really listen, we can have a good shot at hearing it.

Stephen: Man . . . that is a powerful story. [*Pause*] One of the central concepts of this book is the discussion of the soul. Do you believe in the soul, and what does that mean to you?

Loren: Yes, I really do. In fact, the older I've gotten, the more I do believe in it. It goes back to my belief system that there is a breath of life. There is an intelligence at work, but we also know from experience that breath disappears at some point. Where does it go? What happens to it?

Some people call that the spirit, the breath of life, the soul. This creative force we call God. I don't think any of us can prove it, only from our own experiences, but I have come to accept the conclusion that this is a temporary life here in the physical world. How can I really understand love in a perfect world—this Heaven—if I never ever see the opposite of what that is. There is power in that knowledge. I believe the soul is my connection to this vibration, this energy we call God.

Stephen: Do you think in terms of working in communities of need or working with a group of adolescents in a group home, whatever the community, that part of your work has to do with your soul connecting with others? Or finding a connection or having a way to help others find their own connection to the soul. Is there a part of that in your work?

Loren. Yes, there is. I do believe we are all connected. What I do does affect other people. Yes, I think my faith and the soul connection is real. Therefore, I think character matters. How I am accepting or not accepting. It will allow me the privilege of some form of inspiration to influence someone in a profound or inspiring way. I am not interested in changing them or controlling them but providing some inspiration for volitional change. I think that is a big part of that work.

Stephen: A lot of people are making great impact with those they can touch or inspire, but sometimes when we step back and look at the broader challenges of our society and we ask if we are moving in the right direction or wrong direction, how do we tip the scale? That's what this book is really about. What we are talking about is important and profound, but if it's kept in isolation, and we don't find a way to connect on a broader level, we won't see the change that most of us want to see. How do we tip the scale to going from impacting a few to impacting the majority and making real change in the areas we want to see, whether that's poverty, crime, abuse, homelessness, or whatever we want to see changed?

Loren: I have found that most people that are doing this kind of work in communities are bold people. They are confident. They feel a purpose, but they are also humble. That humility is not a weakness. It's the idea is that

I am one person. I have to ask myself, am I that person that can inspire a better world? If not, I need to back up and work on me first. I believe the reality of community change all has the same foundation, and that is about people. If we can get to, first of all, our children, the next ones coming up, to be thinkers and not reflectors of someone else's thought, to be people of value, not religious dogma, but values of character, I believe that is where consciousness begins to rise. As challenging as I see our world, let alone our country, our consciousness can be raised, but all of us have to do our part. To be that model to both adults and children . . . to be that model of a higher consciousness. To me, that's what Jesus, Buddha, Gandhi—the list goes on—the great masters I think taught and tried to get across to people: the idea of seeing people through a lens of love as opposed to a lens of fear. Consciousness will be raised. I thought many times, haven't we, as a nation, now seen enough of the Rambo, enough killing? Haven't we seen enough of war to know that's not where we want to send our children, our boys and now our girls, into? So to raise this consciousness on a community level, we all need to be willing to step to the plate and be that model of genuine love. I know that sounds very cliché and very simple. It's not simple. Love is not sex. Love is not emotion wrapped up in caring for somebody. It's a part of it, but that's not love at the bottom line. One of the things that has inspired me is that Jesus taught, "By your love they will know you are mine." You are part of this source. I do think we are seeing more people moving away from the fundamental religions that promote the belief in Hell and guilt and that type of thing and really get down to the basics of getting into the trenches, understanding love and trying to live. We have too much that divides us. Everyone claims to have the truth. What do I need to do as a human being? We have all this noise, and we can't see the commonalities that are very powerful. What does my heart tell me that I need to do to be a giver, a supporter to inspire? Don't we need to take care of one another? That we are our brother's and sister's keepers.

Stephen: In all the years of your work, going back to the leaf analogy . . . you have been in a lot of settings and leadership roles. You have done a lot of work with troubled youth, young men and women. What has kept you resilient, committed, and as passionate as when you started years ago?

Loren: I'll start with a mind-set first of all. The thing that keeps me motivated is when I see kids who are labeled as troubled, severely emotionally disturbed, diagnosed with conduct disorder, or even victims of sex slavery. It doesn't matter how kids are betrayed or neglected. When I see them face to face, I see the potential inside of them. I say to myself,

Loren, what can I do to help them to see that potential. They need some man to put their arm around them and say, "Son, I care for you. Let's talk." Same thing for the girls, a man to put his arm around them with no other intentions or hidden agenda to manipulate them sexually and just to say "I love you" genuinely. To help them dream again. These kids have stopped dreaming. As long as I feel and think that way—and I pray about it and meditate about it often, but until that changes—I am all in. That's number 1. Number 2 is that I have a great partner. I have known people that are single in this work, and I wonder where they get their support, inspiration, and love. I am very blessed to have a wife that is on the same wavelength as I am. That really is a blessing. More importantly, the bottom line is that I sense that I am an eternal spirit.

Stephen: Tell me what you mean by that?

Loren: I believe that this body that we look at is temporary, but the breath of life was given to it that made it a living being and gave it that spark—a soul and spirit. I believe this source is itself life energy. To take on a human body is a privilege, and along with that comes a profound responsibility. What quality of a person am I going to become? I believe I am an eternal spirit, and when I am through here, I will return to that source.

CHAPTER 4

Holy Sparks Revealed

Happiness cannot be traveled to, owned, earned, worn or consumed. Happiness is the spiritual experience of living every minute with love, grace, and gratitude.
—Denis Waitley

In the book *God Is a Verb*, by Rabbi David A. Cooper, the soul is explained as "a primordial pattern that can be described as a mirror image of us in another dimension . . . it is like a mirror that reflects shape, like an unusual X-ray mirror that shows our spiritual substance." This fascinated me when I first read it not only because the concept of the soul has always intrigued me but also because Rabbi Cooper was a scholar of Jewish and Kabalistic teaching as well as of Eastern religion, philosophy, and spiritual practices, which I have also studied for many years.

I have been a student and teacher of qigong meditation and Chinese martial arts and philosophy for over twenty-five years. Having not been raised in Jewish religious traditions, I had found my own spiritual path through Eastern teachings and the study of qigong, tai chi chuan, hsing-i chuan, Taoist philosophy, and other systems of Chinese gongfu. It was in my late thirties that I began to explore Judaism and some of the more mystical teachings of my religious and cultural background. It was in this book by Rabbi David Cooper where I found a connection between my current spiritual practices and my Jewish ancestry. While various forms of spirituality are found in many religious systems and practices, it was Rabbi Cooper's eloquent explanations of the connection between Jewish teachings from Kabbalah and Eastern philosophy that I found captivating.

His explanation of basic biblical references such as the Garden of Eden, Adam and Eve, and the story of creation truly fascinated me and helped me realize a new way of looking at some of our basic foundational Judeo-Christian beliefs. In this example, the story of Adam and Eve, as Rabbi Cooper describes it, was misread and poorly interpreted when translated from the original Aramaic, an ancient Hebrew script. In the common biblical story, Adam and Eve had been created as two separate beings in which the female literally came from the male's rib. The story continues with Eve being easily tempted by evil in the garden represented by the serpent. Eve then shared the forbidden fruit with Adam, thus cursing humanity for eternity. We know this in Christian theology as original sin. This biblical story has been one of many foundational frameworks and ethos for how Judeo-Christian culture and society has interpreted and understood faith, morality, good and evil, gender, law, and governance for thousands of years.

In the original Aramaic, as described by Cooper, Adam and Eve are more accurately described as a whole, two aspects of a common duality, one being. In essence, a similar concept to yin and yang in Eastern Taoist theory, where one is of the other and the other is of the one. Two halves of a whole. They are both masculine and feminine, soft and hard, light and dark simultaneously. This is a difficult concept to grasp in Western society. In Western philosophy and conceptual frameworks, femininity equates to weakness, masculinity equates to strength, darkness equates to evil, and lightness equates to purity. Good and evil have been firmly rooted in our psyche as opposing forces conflicted and in opposition with each other. These concepts have framed Western civilization and have helped, unfortunately, to create the inequality and divisiveness that we have seen in our culture and society for many generations—from the crusades to colonialism and Jim Crow. I believe that this example helps to explain how we can lose our way and confuse our own history and theology through human interpretation and misrepresentation. We have been taken from the path of being balanced and centered as human beings.

Our human interpretations of the word of God, in this example, have metaphysically divided our spiritual selves in two. We have been pulled away from our center and led astray by our own human failings. In essence, our internal search for fulfillment and peace could be said to be a search for our lost and divided soul. If we embraced the concept of having both a masculine and feminine nature, of being light and dark, good and evil simultaneously, if we realized the power of our full spiritual center, if as human beings we were truly balanced and able to see the fulfillment and unification of our soul and our connection to the larger universe, how might history and the world have evolved differently?

Rabbi Cooper goes on to describe the concept of "Raising Holy Sparks" through a famous sixteenth-century Jewish mystic by the name of Isaac Luria. Luria was said to be an extremely influential theologian and scholar who, according to Cooper, "changed the course of Judaism." Luria said, "There is no sphere of existence, including organic and inorganic nature, that is not filled with holy sparks which are mixed with the *kelipot* (husks) and need to be separated from them and lifted up." My understanding of this concept is that these holy sparks are within and around us, and we have the ability to share and receive these "sparks" every day we are in existence. These holy sparks are manifested by how we interact, communicate, support, love, honor, and cherish one another. In simple acts of "loving kindness" and an understanding of our higher consciousness, we can provide these sparks, "this light" to one another. It is through these simple acts of love and kindness that we become closer to the true nature of our soul or what some may call the Holy Ghost, God, and our deeper spiritual selves. Indeed, our understanding of our unique place and purpose in the universe itself.

In October of 2015, I experienced the loss of my father. At the age of seventy-six, he was suffering from heart disease and kidney failure. I was with him many of the last days of his life. He was in hospice care and was very aware that he had only weeks to live. Though his physical body was dying, frail from the low blood flow and toxins in his system, his mind was sharp and clear until the last few days of his life. He was a brilliant man: a scientist, physician, history buff, lover of classical music, and a complete pragmatist and atheist. If he could not smell, taste, or touch it, he did not believe in it. It would only be validated by scientific method and accepted research.

One of the stories I most recall in this regard was a shared dream that my mother and father had when they first moved into their Evanston home in 1970. My grandfather, Robert Vick, had died before I was born from a heart attack when my father was a very young man in his early twenties. Nonetheless, in 1970, years after his death, he visited my parents at their new home. My father and mother both recall waking up one summer evening to the sound of a door slamming on their porch by their bedroom. They both stood up in bed immediately, looked at each other with wide eyes and said, "Did you hear that?" They proceeded to share with each other that they had both had a dream of Robert visiting them in their bedroom and wishing them well in their new home. He left the room with a slam of the screen door waking, both of my parents simultaneously. Both had heard the same noise. Both had experienced the exact same dream of my grandfather. As they recalled to me, they both sat in bed for thirty minutes in shock, reflecting on their shared experience, trying to find some sense of rationality and explanation. There was none. In my mind, I knew they were visited by the spirit of my grandfather, welcoming them to their new home and wishing them well.

When I would question my father about this shared dream and its implications, he would say, "Steve, I don't want to think about it." I would ask him if there was any logical and/or scientific explanation for two separate people having the exact same dream at the exact time and being woken together by the same unexplainable sound.

I asked him, "Don't you want to explore this and understand what it is?"

His response fascinated me, both because it so deviated from my own interest but also because I believe it also challenged his scientific mind that was taught to search for answers and honor discovery. He said, "Steve, it's like a crumpled paper ball that I want to throw away in the corner of the room and never look at again."

I never forgot this story. It is one of the stories in my family that I wanted to understand and learn more about, but I had no educational or religious context for qualifying this dream or looking into the connotations to exploring my spirituality, the afterlife, and the human relationship to our soul.

In those last days with my father, there were a few things he shared with me that I know made him very pleased. They were his "holy sparks" in the form of gifts that in his own life gave him so much pleasure. I believe that in the last few days of his life, he said the words, "I love you" more than the entirety of my forty-five years of knowing him. Two days before he died, he asked me to go up to his closet in his bedroom on the second floor and bring down two of his suits that no longer fit him due to old age and severe weight loss. One suit was a beautiful double-breasted dark blue pin-striped from the early '80s and the other a dark gray that was cut like it could have been worn by Humphrey Bogart in the 1940s. I brought them down, stood in front of his bed, and, in a low frail voice, he asked me to try them on. I went into the washroom to change. They both fit beautifully, almost as if they had been made for me by a tailor. As I stood in front of him in his hospice bed, he seemed to jump out of his own skin with excitement. His aching emaciated frame momentarily did not bother him. He was full of pride and true joy at the fit of his old suits on his youngest son. I almost heard him cheer with excitement.

These gifts were symbolic of my father and how he treated people. Always attentive, caring, generous, and giving of himself selflessly. Though somewhat antisocial with those he did not know well, with those he loved, he would give the world. His kindness and compassion for his family, friends, and those in his care as a physician of forty years was truly remarkable. He died that next day in the early hours of the morning. I remember the call at four thirty in the morning from my mother. A call I had been expecting for many years. Sobbing quietly, she said, "Daddy is gone. Come on over when you can." When I arrived at the house an hour later, the hospice workers were there waiting for the funeral home to come pick up his body. He was covered in a white bedsheet. All was very still and quiet in his den where he had spent the last weeks of his life. When the funeral workers came, they asked me to leave the room, as they would have to move his body from the bed to the gurney to transport him. I told them that I would stay, and we shut the double doors to hide from the view of my mother. His body was white and cold, almost rubberlike, empty. I sometimes regret seeing him this way, but I have realized that it was a gift. I had seen my father's body empty of all the greatness and passion that he was. I knew immediately that he was much, much more than a simple physical presence in the world. In fact, his physical body was just that—a vessel carrying an amazing, brilliant, and compassionate soul through the world. That soul had not changed. It had simply moved on, left its physical body and metamorphosed as a butterfly from a cocoon.

My father has been one of the great teachers in my life. He taught me of compassion, caring, hard work, integrity, responsibility, and love. Though he would never describe it as such, he taught me of sharing and receiving "holy sparks." His death still feels very fresh in my mind. We buried his cremated remains in our garden, where he spent hundreds of hours tending his tomato plants and rose bushes. Strangely, I still feel as if he is on a work trip or vacation and will be returning home sometime soon. I know the loss of my father will always be present in my mind as a pivotal moment in my life that will forever be remembered. Though he never believed it possible in his physical life, I speak to his soul periodically and know that he watches over me and is proud.

The concept of "acts of loving kindness" is so powerful yet so simple and clear. How we interact and treat one another, those in our family, our friends, our neighborhood, and our community, is so relevant to the success of the work of community development and collective spiritual health. It begs to ask the question: what does it really mean to live in a community together? In order to elevate our connection and commitment to one another as human beings, we must learn about each other's needs and hopes for the future. We must respect our uniqueness and value our differences while acknowledging our shared humanity and spiritual connectivity. We have to find a way to move beyond fearing one another and embrace our shared need for love, compassion, healing, hope, and opportunity to become more interconnected and transformational souls.

Maybe it is too simplistic, but let's start by meeting with one another, talking honestly about our joy and pain, listening to our different concerns and dreams for our children. Try to understand the life experience of another and walk in their shoes momentarily. Hopefully, we can take the time to be thoughtful, empathetic, compassionate, and concerned while participating in giving and receiving acts of "loving kindness." It might go a long way.

CHAPTER 5

Charles Perry

Mississippi and Washington DC

I imagine one of the reasons people cling to their hates so stubbornly is because they sense, once hate is gone, they will be forced to deal with pain.
—James Baldwin

I met Charles Perry about fifteen years ago while working as a consultant with the AmeriCorps VISTA program. A branch of the Corporation for National and Community Service. VISTA stood for Volunteers in Service to America and was promoted as our national peace corps. We were trainers and facilitators who helped guide new recruits in their Pre-Service Orientation. These VISTAs were made up of people from every walk of life who were committing a year of service with the goal of reducing poverty in struggling communities through working with grassroots organizations and community advocates trying to implement change. Charles later invited me to join a contract with the Department of Justice known as Weed and Seed, focused on youth development and providing avenues for youth voice and leadership. We currently work together for the Center for Neighborhood Enterprise, providing resources, tools, and technical assistance enhancing community empowerment, collaboration, and economic revitalization. This interview was conducted on a long rainy drive from Topeka, Kansas, to the Kansas City Airport after a week of training and group facilitation.

Stephen: Tell me little about yourself: who you are, where you come from, and what you do in the community?

Charles: I was born in Lake City, Florida, which is a small agrarian town. My mom was a housemaid earning $20 a week. My grandmother was also a housemaid earning $25 a week taking care of someone else's children. So I basically grew up with my granddaddy in the house. He was a lumberjack of sorts. My dad, while he was in the town, didn't live with us and had two or three jobs. I understood why later, as he had several children and a lot of child support payments. I grew up in this town with a lot of love. I was the only child in the house. I was raised as an only child as far as my mother was concerned. They got me everything I wanted. They put all their resources into me. Of course, my dad helped. There was never a time I needed something that he didn't provide. So even though he wasn't in the house, he was indeed a provider, and I knew he was a provider. I grew up and became a teenager working in the tobacco fields, which helped develop my work ethic. Actually, I began washing windows for the lady my mom worked for. She owned a children's clothing shop, so my mom didn't have to provide me with clothes, as I got them for free from the shop. Up till when I was thirteen or fourteen, all my clothes came from this shop. I was in a poor condition but didn't know I was poor.

Stephen: What year was this?

Charles: This was 1954 through about 1968. In 1968, I became in tune with the race consciousness of the country with Martin Luther King. I first remember when JFK was assassinated when I was in the fourth grade, but that didn't hit me as much as Martin Luther King's death in April 4, 1968. There were a lot of race riots in Florida and definitely Lake City, Florida. So I became a race conscious individual.

Stephen: How old were you at that point with the riots?

Charles: I was about fourteen. So I was becoming an adolescent. In high school, I was always active—played in the band, played the trumpet, in the cub scouts and boy scouts. That helped shape me as a person. The other mentor in my life was my invisible uncle in my house.

He was so loved by my mom and grandma, there wasn't a week that went by where they didn't talk about Uncle Sam. He stayed in the army for thirty years. Even more so than my daddy, he became a hero and a deciding factor for me to enter the military even though he wasn't in the house. He was my role model for what I wanted to do when I grew up.

Stephen: So tell me about your military experience.

Charles: I went in at the age of seventeen because I wanted to escape poverty. Like I said, Lake City was an agrarian city. I did not see myself working the fields as an adult, nor could I see myself working in the chalk mines. There were chalk mines there for the company that made Kaopectate. They also had an aircraft stripping plant and a house trailer manufacturer. I knew I didn't want to do any of those things.

Stephen: Limited opportunities.

Charles: Limited opportunities, so I jumped in the military and stayed for twenty-two years. I retired at the age of thirty-eight and was a happy camper. I was first stationed in Montana, then in the republic of Korea for a year, moved to Georgia for twelve years, working in security personnel, and then my last six years in Washington DC.

Stephen: I know you have worked for the Center for Neighborhood Enterprise for many years and in communities for a long time. How did you make the transition from the military to more focused on community needs and serving local folks?

Charles: I had been praying . . . When you're in the military for your nineteen years, you can apply for retirement. You know, I had forgot to mention I had been to church all my life. I forgot to mention that part. I got baptized at age six in Lake City, Florida, behind the hospital I was born in. It was at Shiloh Baptist Church, and whether consciously or subconsciously, I was destined to serve the "least of these." I didn't know exactly how to do that, so what happened for me was to take a risk and become a self-employed person. I had a pension check and health insurance, and so I decided to become a self-employed consultant in 1992. I came across some literature on the Center for Neighborhood Enterprise and made it my point to call them and say, "I want to work for you. How can I make that happen?" They called me one day and said they were interested in talking to me about a consulting gig, and the rest is history.

Stephen: How many years have you been with the Center for Neighborhood Enterprise?

Charles: I have been with them for twenty-two years as a consultant. I've also had other jobs working with HIV/AIDS and the Center for Substance Abuse and Prevention as well as other government consulting jobs.

Stephen: These are all in impoverished or struggling communities?

Charles: These communities were impoverished, drug infested, alcoholic communities, so the federal government was trying to find ways to solve these problems.

Stephen: I have to back up a minute. You said something that I think is really important. You mentioned that when you were leaving the military, you prayed to God, and you were told to work for the "least of these." That's not very common. Where did that come from? Why did that manifest?

Charles: I would have to say my momma and grandmomma always kept me in church. I believe in the power of prayer, and I knew that I didn't know the answer, so I asked for guidance. Let me just say I was the prodigal son. During that time, I had been married a few times, children from three women. Strapped with child support.

Stephen: Busy.

Charles: Busy. I had my first child at seventeen before I joined the military. My first child was born the year I graduated from high school. I got married two times after that. I prayed even though I was the prodigal son. If you know the story in the Bible, before the son came to his senses he has to eat with the pigs. He had to go through trials and tribulations from his own doing. I could have chased the dollar, but I wanted to be guided by what God wanted me to do.

Stephen: That leads me to my next question: how does faith play a role, not only in the communities you serve but also the work you do with the community?

Charles: I think there is a war out here between good and evil. I would rather be in the army of the good. I pray every day. I might not go to the altar, but I pray in my car, wherever, because God is omniscient and omnipresent. He has taught me to work with those in need, he drives me. Like a preacher might say they have a calling. This happens to be my calling. God has never failed me and never left me. I have been broke, but it was of my own doing. Opportunities would always arise. I was sent to the right person or right place at the right time.

Stephen: Do you think with the work you do around the country and what the topic you just shared is a critical piece? Do you believe the empowering of people with faith and the belief in God is a critical piece to change these communities?

Charles: I think so. I have empathy for the common good of people. Perhaps to my own challenge, but I have a basic belief that people are good in nature. So when I meet you, I am going to assume the good things in you. I help people tap into that goodness and help themselves and show them how to help others. CNE and other groups I work with in Mississippi are the same. People on SNAP benefits, the poor, HIV/AIDS population, etc., are people society shun, whom society frown upon. I am just trying to do well by doing something good.

Stephen: Do you believe there is a soul, and if so, how would you describe it?

Charles: To me, our soul is our consciousness. You have to be linked to both good and bad soul and connected to the greater universe. God put us on the earth to serve others through goodwill and help mankind fight evil. I'm not sure how good people can stand by and let this evil take control.

Stephen: Is the soul inherently good?

Charles: I think the soul is inherently good. But I have to go back to the sociologist's perspective where "the hand that rocks the cradle rules the world." I happened to have had faith believing parents and grandparents. Even my dad, who wasn't a bad man, he just had some issues with women, but he always treated me well. I think the soul is an internal thing. Even when your subconsciousness allows a bad thought in your mind, your conscious mind keeps it in control and in check. Hey, I am a wretch undone. I will be the first to tell you. I am imperfect, but my consciousness and my soul guide me. There is an interesting warfare that goes on inside of the soul. Not to hate. You know, when people say or do something that is against you, you must forgive them to not become hateful. Your countenance can become hateful, and your disposition becomes hateful. I think the soul, in and of itself, is the interaction between your conscious and unconscious mind.

Stephen: Do you believe when we leave our body that the soul continues on?

Charles: I believe our soul is implanted into our children and grandchildren. The values, attitudes, norms, beliefs are implanted into them. The soul lives on through them . . . through your work. I asked people the other day, "What is their legacy?" They should look at the things they can do to assist others. Many people use their writing, books, songs, and art to have their legacy carry on.

Stephen: What would you say are your greatest challenges and barriers to being successful?

Charles: Your health is the first thing that leads to wealth. You can have all the wealth in the word, but without health, how can you enjoy it? I have diabetes and hypertension. I need to be conscious of what I eat, the frequency that I visit the doctor. How we eat, overindulging, drinking liquor . . . all these things affect our health and ability to be successful.

Stephen: Do you think there is a parallel in the communities we serve?

Charles: Most definitely. In the communities we serve, you have people that have examples of illness related to alcoholism, drug addiction, etc., but their consciousness does not pull them out. They have not had the background or role models to help create that consciousness. I had a strong background with how I was raised by my mother and grandmother.

Stephen: Doing the work you do in these communities, being a leader yourself, what do you think leadership in these communities needs to look like? Do leaders have to come from within the community for us to see sustainable change?

Charles: I think that the ideal leader in the community is a pastor or preacher. The black church, for example, is an institution that has helped black people through slavery, Jim Crow, through segregation, through integration, this whole reformation, and new age. I think I have learned a lot of my leadership mannerisms from preachers, to be honest. Preachers are humble yet straightforward. They are empathetic yet know how to chastise.

Stephen: We all know there are some leaders, but usually there seems to be a lot of followers. How do we find those leaders in a sea of followers?

Charles: My grandmother used to always say, "Birds of a feather flock together." So she taught me early on to associate with a bird of the feather of Christ. To stay away from people who stole, fought, killed, or gambled. One of the reasons I don't like gambling now, even though it is legal in many places, is that I was double dog dared to go close to the pool hall growing up.

Stephen: Double dog dared?

Charles: Yes, sir. In other words, get my butt beat. A pool hall in Lake City, Florida, is where people got killed for not paying their debts.

Stephen: It's that consciousness again from your upbringing. This is a recurring theme in our conversation . . . Question . . . this work we do is heavy work. Many of the people we work with are dealing with serious trauma and emotional challenges. How do you keep yourself positive and resilient?

Charles: I had to learn how to let go and not be so controlling. I think I learned a lot of that control I need from the military. I think of the prayer of serenity, "Lord give me the courage to change the things that I can, the serenity to accept the things I can't, but more importantly, the wisdom to know the difference." For me, I can control the internal environment but can't control the external environment. I have to look at what we do. I know I can't live someone else's life for them. It's up to people to make the change for themselves. I can provide people with framework and skills, but they have to make the changes.

Stephen: Out of all the work you have done and the places you have been, what is one of the examples where your work made impact and change, where you saw something really powerful in an individual or community?

Charles: Outside of my children, I would have to say there has been a continuum of good work and goodwill. I may not know evidence immediately but for a few instances. When someone you have touched comes back to you years later just to say hello. To communicate what they have done and what you did for them. Of late, it has been in the State of Mississippi after working with kids who come back years later after finishing law school or graduate school and sending a message of thanks that I made a difference in their lives.

Stephen: Any final thoughts or feelings about the work you have been doing over the course of your life?

Charles: Legacy . . . to be able to pass on the experiences and passion for serving others to my children. That to me is the greatest gift I can give. Legacy. To continue to do what we do. If people can just hook in on their contributions to society. The whole world is a stage. You are an actor in it. You think nobody's watching, but God is watching. I think that you have to reflect on the impact we make on this earth. You need to be in tune with that. There is a hymnal that says, "Lord guide my mind, guide my feet, while I run this race, 'cause I sure don't want this race to be in vain." When God asks, "How did you treat my people? What did you do for the least of these?" What will you say to him? Were you kind? Were you helpful or destructive? Did you close your fist or open your hand? How will you answer him? What is your legacy?

CHAPTER 6

A Faith-Based Approach

The thing to do, it seems to me, is to prepare yourself so you can be a rainbow in somebody else's cloud. Somebody who may not look like you. May not call God the same name you call God—if they call God at all. I may not dance your dances or speak your language. But be a blessing to somebody. That's what I think.
—Maya Angelou

During our summit introductions and welcomes on our first day with the Center for Neighborhood Enterprise, it was clear that we had a strong representation of local pastors and preachers from the Kansas City community. In fact, the event was headed by the Kansas Department of Children and Families Faith-Based Initiative, sponsored by Republican governor Sam Brownback. Faith plays a strong role in resiliency in many of our economically depressed and struggling communities. The American spirituals and songs of resiliency are heard from hymnals and gospel choirs in our churches and places of worship across the country, especially the South. The history of this voice and musical tradition has a long and complex history coming out of the struggles in the agricultural South and the journey of many black people to a supposed freedom in the Northern urban centers. The belief in Jesus Christ and a deep spiritual presence of faith, resiliency, and hope is often brought up as a critical role in the salvation of our communities but is often tied to the dogmatic teaching of evangelical faiths and the exclusionary attitude toward the nonbeliever.

I have always struggled with this conflict between faith and inclusion. Even in a committed group of leaders, struggling to find solutions to common community ills, the face of prejudice, intolerance, and discrimination raises its head. Why do faith and belief so often walk hand in hand with prejudice and intolerance?

The struggle between sacred and secular approaches to community development has been very interesting in our country. The separation of church and state is an interesting contradiction in community empowerment work. Churches, temples, mosques, and other places of worship have always been an anchor for those in need and a safe haven for people struggling with homelessness, addiction, hunger, and poverty. Many of our soup kitchens, clothing closets, and supportive services operate out of the basements and back rooms of our houses of worship. Likewise, since the new deal, government support and safety net services such as SNAP, social security, and child care subsidies have played an important role in providing support to our most needy.

Consequently, I would suggest that it is not faith and spirituality that are causing challenges and conflicts but religious and governmental institutions—and the dogmatic practices within which they operate. Faith and a spiritual connection to a deeper purpose and soul consciousness are not monopolized by one religious tradition or another. I would argue that, in fact, most religious scriptures and systems of belief are connected through a shared emphasis on compassion, goodness, kindness, love, and peacefulness.

If this is indeed the case, then where is there a conflict? The conflict arises when faith-based organizations and religious institutions choose to serve only a certain group of people and exclude others due to their religious beliefs or when these institutions evangelize their faith and require participation in order to receive services. Likewise, when government or private institutions make assumptions about the motives of faith-based institutions, we see disconnection and resistance to partnerships even when there is a common community or cause.

The term "faith-based" often causes great concern and debate as we discuss how to assist struggling communities. This is due to our varying interpretations of faith and what it means to be faithful. What are we being faithful to? Is it the word of God? Is it Jesus, Vishnu, Allah, Buddha, the Great Mother? The spiritual thread of kindness, compassion, love, community connection, and harmony are present in all these teachings.

These elements connect all these as well as other traditions. How does the atheist define and practice faith?

I would suggest our soul is not bound by the names, traditions, and practices of the belief system we follow but by our actions and deeds as we walk through our lives on this earth. If I was a righteous person, kind, sharing of love, and light in this world, regardless of my tradition, would I be denied a place in Heaven? Some might say yes. Our spiritual beliefs and soul purposefulness is the place that connects us and elevates our common ground as human beings. Even those that do not believe in a higher power, those we name atheists, would honor and value the principles of goodness, kindness, compassion, harmony with others, and love. Our challenge is to start finding the things that connect us, that are shared across cultures and religious traditions. It is not a matter of changing our beliefs or traditions to fit another's. It is the idea of finding common ground, a shared vision, and a common spiritual purpose.

The idea of finding common ground has always been difficult for us, whether individuals or institutions. Nonreligious organizations as well as our faith-based providers have not done a good job of partnering and developing collaborative relationships. There are certainly examples where a community fabric has been woven, and the connection between institutions has developed and created strong connectivity and elevated the ability to provide service to individuals and communities in need. However, it is rare; and most community providers, whether faith-based or secular, have not developed substantial, long-lasting relationships of any kind. The concepts of communication and collaboration are key factors in moving our discussion of community empowerment and transformational leadership forward. In fact, these are the very conversations that can begin to shed light on the deeper challenges that face our most underserved and disenfranchised communities and why many of our local safety net organizations as well as state and federal services are simply not meeting the challenge.

One excellent example of strategic collaboration and partnership development occurred while working in the Humboldt Park community on the Northwest Side of Chicago in the early 1990s. Three organizations— Association House of Chicago, Casa Central, and Erie Neighborhood House—were all struggling to fill their youth enrollment in their respective after-school programs. On the Northwest Side of Chicago in the West Town/Humboldt Park community, there is a very dense population of youth ages ten to eighteen. All three of these grassroots agencies targeted this age group to provide safe after-school activities that were engaging and provided mentoring, cultural content, and a positive connection to adults. The crime and violence in the community was high, with a dropout percentage of about 50 percent from the local high schools. Each organization provided similar youth services, but after-school programming was differentiated between art and music, boxing and recreational sports, and tutoring and homework assistance.

I was involved with one of the organizations, and there was some frustration that there was such low attendance. Most of the services offered were free. They were subsidized by state and city grants. It was obviously not a cost issue that kept people away. Our youth program director had surveyed the youth and knew that the programs offered were of interest. It took some time, but leaders of the three organizations finally began to communicate and realized all three programs were equally suffering from low attendance. I recall that after some focus groups with the youth and parents, it turned out the reason kids were not attending was due to gang violence and the boundaries that existed in the neighborhood. These were invisible lines that outsiders knew nothing of, but the kids and families in the neighborhood knew exactly where and when they could go out. It was simply too dangerous. Parents did not want to send their kids to the programming due to very real safety concerns.

After putting their heads together, an old bus was secured by one of the organizations and the letters "YOU" were scrolled in bright colors along the side of the white school bus. It stood for Youth Options Unlimited. This bus began driving back and forth between the three agencies and the neighboring communities between the hours of 3:00 p.m. and 8:00 p.m. It was miraculous. All three of the programs began to fill up, and parents were calling in to get their children in the YOU program. It was not interest or desire but safety and a common problem of transportation that kept the kids away. This seems like a simple solution, but it wasn't until dedicated and committed leaders reached out to their competition and realized they could all benefit from a deeper level of communication and collaboration. This program went on for years, and though it has changed and evolved over time to meet the needs of its constituents, the YOU program is still in operation today on the Northwest Side of Chicago twenty-five years after it was created.

This concept of shared need and collaborative programming is not a difficult concept to understand in words, but in practice, it is much harder to see manifest as the YOU programming did in the early '90s. It takes visionary, passionate leaders with a commitment to community, and family to see these types of opportunities arise. These are the harbormasters. The local leaders who know what is needed and create viable solutions to local challenges. Why is this so hard to see happen across the social service landscape? How can faith-based organizations and institutions be connected with local secular NPOs in these ways?

Too often, organizational leaders, especially in the larger institutions, are out of touch with the deeper needs of the neighborhood, front-line staff, clients, families, and youth in a community. Program directors and staff who are meeting the needs of the community must be given adequate resources and local control. Leadership often does not allow power and authority to trickle down to those with the most knowledge and understanding of the local issues. This can make it very difficult to operate effectively. When you are given a set of prescribed revenue goals and funding guidelines that don't quite meet the needs of the people you are serving, it can become very difficult to be effective. It takes special leaders that can lead from behind and listen to their staff and direct appropriate support and funding opportunities to the needs of the local providers. These are the transformational leaders who can bring true change to our most struggling communities. Those who are in positions of power in our institutions and organizations must recognize it is only through the empowerment of others that will allow true creativity, innovation, and engagement to thrive and grow successfully.

Just as a struggling, homeless, drug-addicted person may be seen as "lost," many of our so-called leaders and those who have been in places of authority and power have also been "lost" through their arrogance, greed, ignorance, ego, as well as financial and administrative mismanagement. The finding of one's "soul" and becoming balanced and whole can be a personal and an organizational and institutional journey. Institutional racism, poor fiscal responsibility, nepotism, a culture of oppression, and distrust are all aspects of an organization or institution that is spiritually lost. How can we hope to alleviate community challenges and disparity if the very organizations and institutions that are held up as leaders and pioneers in the field are not able to recognize and address their own challenges and faults?

Many organizations and faith-based institutions have some of the same institutional challenges that we see in the local, state, and federal government. Often, there is a network of organizations that seem to repeatedly receive funding and are always at the table, regardless of their effectiveness, data, and impact. Many times, dollars follow relationships; and more often than not, these organizations are not looking for harbormasters and community leaders to support and galvanize but are serving their own agenda, financial bottom line, and organizational self-edification. The challenges of race, class power, and privilege in our country play out in the arena of social services and programming for those in need. The majority of the billions of dollars being pumped into poverty initiatives is going to pay for the providers rather than the poor themselves. There are many examples of churches and organizations going into communities where there is no real representation and leadership from the community within that church or organizational structure. The concept of leading from behind and looking for the leaders and support systems that already exist becomes such a crucial aspect of creating real and lasting change.

I recently attended a conference where an all-white panel representing a confederation of church organizations was sharing their work in a struggling community. They were passionate about their mission and sincere regarding their belief in evangelizing the savior of the community through God. This community was very diverse. Fifty percent black, twenty-five percent Latino, and the rest mixed between white and Native American. My first thought was how can this panel be all white? If you are serving a diverse community, is there no relevant voice other than a white one? Even the member of the panel from the community was white. The presentation screamed of paternalism, white privilege and some strange modern-day evangelical throwback to colonialism. Spiritual and religious traditions and institutions, faith, and the belief in a shared vision for the future is essential for communities in need. We must, however, allow the harbormasters and the diamonds that already exist in the community to shine and flourish. Providing support structures, grants, infrastructure, and technical assistance to these leaders and letting them lead is a necessity. Local leaders must navigate and drive the vision. It's okay to fill the gas tank, but you don't have to assume you get to drive or even sit in the front seat. It may even be best if you don't get in the car at all.

The undertones of race and class politics play out here, sometimes in very overt ways. These are the difficult conversations to have because they challenge the status quo and threaten the balance of power and place that power, decision making, and money in the hands of those closest to the poor themselves. Whether secular or faith-based, there is a need to take a look introspectively and organizationally at how interaction, communication, funding, and resource allocation is handled and ultimately distributed in communities of need. If we do not change the way we are funding community-based programming, how we can work collaboratively across systems, and rethink how leadership and vision is manifested, we will unfortunately perpetuate a system that has been ineffective for decades.

CHAPTER 7

Jewel Ware,
Chicago, Illinois

*Service is the rent we pay for being. It is the very purpose of
life, and not something you do in your spare time.*
—Marian Wright Edelman

I met Jewel Ware while working for AmeriCorps VISTA about fifteen
years ago. We traveled across the country training VISTA volunteers for
their year of service combating poverty. Since those times, Jewel and I
have worked on various contracts together but also became close friends
as we lived not too far from one another in Chicago. Her daughter, Holly,
began babysitting for my wife and me when our kids were young. Jewel
is compassionate and caring. She is a wonderful mother and has given
not only to her children but also taken in others and cared for them as
her own. She is insightful, intelligent, and extremely talented in working
with people, organizations, and communities. She has a light about her
that shines brightly. Her spirit and soul are ones that touch others in
meaningful and powerful ways. I met Jewel for this interview on a warm,
sunny Thursday afternoon in her turn-of-the-century gray stone building.
We sat talking in the parlor of her West Side Chicago home.

Stephen: Tell me about yourself, who you are, where you came from, and
the work you do. Who is Jewel Ware?

Jewel: [*Laughing*] I am what I call a true Midwesterner. I've lived in the
Midwest my entire life. Chicago, all except two years in Columbus, Ohio.

I've lived on every side of Chicago there is to live—South Side, West Side, and North Side. I have worked on my own as an independent consultant for twenty-seven years. I have a few bumps and bruises, but I'm still standing.

Stephen: Where did you grow up?

Jewel: I had four sisters and three brothers, but I was raised as an only child by my father's mother. My grandmother raised me. I grew up in the '40s on the South Side. Fortieth and Cottage Grove. As a child, the only occupations I wanted to do was in the helping profession. I spent a lot of time in the hospital as a child and thought I wanted to be a nurse. Back then, women didn't think of being doctors.

Stephen: Why were you in the hospital so often?

Jewel: I had polio. I was like the last wave. Depending on the story you hear, I either had the vaccination shot and was exposed, or I didn't have the shot and was exposed. So because I spent so much time in the hospital, I wanted to be a nurse. Although I didn't like shots or blood and quickly realized that wouldn't be a good plan. The second thing I wanted to do was to be a social worker. My undergrad was in social work. The technical term at Northern Illinois was called "children and family services."

Stephen: You said that you spent a lot of time in the hospital with polio, and you wanted to give back and be a helper or healer. I don't want to make assumptions, but do you think that because you were going through a difficult medical issue and challenging situation that you in turn wanted to help others? Or was it something you learned from your father or grandmother? Where did the idea of helping others come from?

Jewel: I would have to say that there is more than one answer. You know how some people go through life and say, "Why me? Why me?" My personal belief is that people cope however they can. For me, it wasn't just the polio. I had a father that was a schizophrenic. I had some other family stuff. For me, how I rationalized being a recipient in all these things in life was that I was strong enough to take it. I remember thinking as a child if I didn't take it, others would have to. I can remember as young as seven or eight thinking these things. The human spirit has to find some rationale, or you can go under. So enduring hardship so someone else wouldn't have to.

Stephen: Even turning it around into a career and continuing to work with people and communities.

Jewel: Anyone who has worked in the social work field knows it can be draining and taxing. I realized child care work was not going to be a long-term place for me. I was intentional. I actually did some work around the skill set that I had. I wanted to impact people in a positive way and still make some income. That's how I came to training and development work and my own consulting business.

Stephen: I would assume enjoying what you do at the same time? You mentioned something about spirituality, that we need to cope with challenges in spiritual ways. Were you raised in any spiritual tradition or faith?

Jewel: My grandmother raised me. She was old school. She only went to the third grade. She didn't have the scholastic background, but she always told me I was going to go to college. I was the first one in my family to go to college. Education was very important to her. She actually died when I was a senior in high school.

Stephen: That's a tough age to experience that. She was like a mother to you, right?

Jewel: [*Pause*] It was never a matter of was I going to college. It was just how it was going to really happen. Momma didn't take me to church too much. I would go to the church across the way on Sundays. I wouldn't say I am religious, but I am a very spiritual person. I'll share a story with you. When I was about ten or eleven, I was going to kill myself. I had gotten pills . . . and so I had decided that my grandmother's' life would have been easier if I wasn't there. I had it all figured out. I had all different pills from all different places. I'm not sure if I had enough to kill myself, but in my mind, I did. I actually had a dream the night before. I had made all these plans and thought everyone's life would be easier. I had this dream about God. He told me not to do it and that I had a lot of things I was supposed to do with my life.

Stephen: This was the night before your suicide plan?

Jewel: It was . . . In my mind then, if God told you to do something, you did it, or else you would go straight to Hell. So I didn't do it. That stuck with me. When I was fifteen, I used to go to a place in Wisconsin called Holy Field. It followed the steps of Jesus. We would go every year as far back as I can remember. Maybe from age six to the age fourteen. We went on this church bus. It was a female minister that prophesied who led the congregation. She would talk to everyone on the bus. I still think about it. This woman said I see you as an adult talking to thousands of people. You are going to have an impact on them. I was like, "What?" As a kid, you don't really get it.

Stephen: Those are powerful stories that changed your life direction . . . Tell me about the work you do now as an adult. Help me understand more about how you impact people and community?

Jewel: This is how I start many of my talks and seminars . . . Every year I get my wedding ring cleaned. Every year, when I get it cleaned, I am amazed how it sparkles and shines. I don't think about how the sparkle got dull through the year. You know . . . you do the dishes, you clean, you get stuff on it that blocks the shine. You just get used to it looking dull. It is only when you shine it that you remember how beautiful it is. I like to think that the work I do and the talks I do with groups is like helping get rid of the "stuff" that blocks your internal glow. A lot of people are carrying false perceptions in their heads. Things that they have been told as children that they still carry with them. I'm taking off a lot of the "stuff" that blocks peoples' effectiveness and success.

Stephen: With all this work and giving and healing. It takes a lot of energy. It can be draining. What do you do to keep yourself motivated and sustained in your work?

Jewel: I like to dance, play cards, relax in the house. I mentally put on a shield. Some people can literally drain you and take all your energy, so I have learned to defend against it with this shield. I have become good at sensing people that can drain me in that way.

Stephen: Earlier, you talked about a few examples of spirituality and faith and some dreams that helped guide you. How does your sense of spirituality help you? You shared the idea of helping others make their light shine. How does this sense of spirituality guide your work?

Jewel: I like to think that it guides everything I do. I believe we are spiritual beings in human form. If you were to ask me what my essence is,

I would say I am joy, light, and laughter. Everyone has a different purpose of being. I know some people who are calming. I can be that way, but when I am in my zone, I know who I am. I like feeling that I leave people in a better place than they were when our paths crossed. For some, that can be a few minutes or an hour. For others, it takes time for things to sink in . . . People need to work through things. My intent is always to leave people in a better place. Being spiritual shows up with me by being authentic. People who have known me for a number of years and seen me in different settings will say I am always me. It's honoring your essence, your soul, or your spirit.

Stephen: That's a great lead-in to my next question. Do you believe in a soul? If you do, how would you describe it?

Jewel: Man, you are making me really think! I'll give you a two-part answer to that question. Something I have been contemplating is soul and spirit as different or the same thing. I'm just going to say soul-spirit. The soul is the container, the holder of all your experiences, all your energy. I do think there are some souls who are more connected than some others to the nonphysical world. If your soul is more connected to the nonphysical realm, you have more insight and wisdom. It's not just what you have accumulated in your lifetime. You are connected to the wisdom of the ages.

Stephen: You were talking about this wisdom, light, connectivity. This larger spiritual realm. Are some people not able to tap into that? Why are some people able to get to a higher sense of self than others? You went through struggle as you shared growing up, but you are able to get connected to this soulfulness. Are some people blocked from that?

Jewel: Good question. I think it goes back to freewill. The Bible says we all have freewill. I think that anyone that is committed and willing to put in the work can access that channel so to speak. If you chose not to, if you live . . . everyone has the capability. I think that our society is so logically and scientifically oriented that some will miss it. I think some people feel the existence is there, but they don't care. They have chosen to go down another path. I believe in God, I believe in freewill, and God doesn't force us to do anything.

Stephen: When we look at the world today . . . it seems like there are just so many challenges so many problems, so many aspects of our human existence contains so much struggle—racism, poverty, criminality, etc. How do we take this stuff you're talking about and make larger-scale impact? How do we take what you are saying, which is powerful stuff, and make larger-scale change? Or can we?

Jewel: First of all, we are talking about shifting the consciousness of the planet . . . Let's just say the United States to keep it local. What are we feeding our spirit or soul? Sometimes I take TV fasts. I need to get away from the negative energy that is broadcast to us. I think most people have more love than they are conscious of. We are not investing in our young people. A lot of children haven't experienced love, so they are not able to show love. There is so much work to do in our country, but I have joy because of people like you. There are so many sparks and embers around the country. People I know who are positive and impactful. People are writing about spirituality and love. There is more information knowledge and insight being shared than I have ever seen before. I would say with the advent of social media, smart phones, Facebook, etc., the technology combined with a greater sense of purpose will help it move forward, but it takes quite a bit of time to turn a large ship.

Stephen: You are very optimistic and positive person. How do you stay hopeful with all the things that are going on around us?

Jewel: That's funny you asked me that. I have had a few people ask me that recently. It's obviously something I need to think more about. If I gave you a short answer it would be, if you don't have hope, what do you have? I think in too many people, especially our young people, hope has been extinguished.

Steve: They are hopeless.

Jewel: When that happens, there is no optimism, no resiliency. I see those as being connected.

Steve: I have to come back full circle. You told me when you were eight or nine, you tried to take your life. You must have felt hopeless then. My mind keeps going back to the dream you had about God. Do you think that people need to have some kind of faith in a higher power to provide some kind of hopefulness?

Jewel: I think everyone needs to believe in something larger than themselves. I see that as being separate from God. For me, I believe in God. Other people believe in Buddha, Allah, etc., but they are still believing in something larger than themselves. There are so many overlaps in the major religions: goodness, peace, love, treating others as you would be treated. If you don't believe in something larger than yourself, it is easier to get depressed. It's easier to become cynical. It's easier to give up. I think there is something after life . . . whatever it is, but I believe in making a difference in this life.

CHAPTER 8

Seeking Out and Deleting Files

This life therefore is not righteousness, but growth in righteousness,
not health, but healing, not being but becoming, not rest but exercise.
We are not yet what we shall be, but we are growing toward it, the
process is not yet finished, but it is going on, this is not the end, but it
is the road. All does not yet gleam in glory, but all is being purified.
—Martin Luther

In my consulting work traveling around the country, training and facilitating seminars and workshops in the area of diversity and inclusion, I have found that before organizations, corporations and institutions can grapple with larger issues of workplace culture, they first must do the work of embracing individual and personal growth and reflection as senior organizational leadership. All organizations and institutions are made up of individual people. It is we, as individual human beings, who bring our ethos and cultural norms to the workplace. It is the CEO, board, or senior leadership, more often than not, who sets the tone and creates the climate. As said so eloquently by author Haim Ginott, "Leaders (teachers) can be a tool of torture or instrument of inspiration."

In a recent role as presenter of diversity and inclusion leadership as a part of the larger supervisory training with the YMCA of Metropolitan Chicago, I took the approach of having people first look at their own bias and how they viewed their environment through their own cultural lenses. How were they as individuals brought up and raised? What values, beliefs, experiences, and morals shaped their identity as children, and who was involved in their teaching and upbringing? Very rarely do we reflect on these issues in a group setting where we can speak honestly about who we are and where we came from. I often use the example of placing a mirror in front of one's face and looking beyond the reflection, deeper into one's heart and consciousness. This is a difficult process and not an easy thing to do. Honesty with oneself and one's self-concept can bring serious emotional responses and, at times, painful memories and experiences from the past.

One of the questions I ask during my sessions is for people to reflect on a time in their early childhood when they were with family at a meal sitting around a table or eating informally. Once that memory is in mind, I ask them to think carefully about who was present in the room, father, mother, aunt, uncle, grandparent. I ask them to focus on the faces of each individual and the conversations that took place. Once everyone has their mind focused, I ask if they ever heard anything said during that meal by a family member that they would now, as an adult, consider inappropriate toward someone's race, ethnicity, gender, sexual orientation, or religion. In almost every workshop, over the last twenty years where I have used this visualization technique, approximately ninety percent of the participants reluctantly raise their hands. I would guess that most of those who didn't raise their hand probably were not comfortable admitting it in public. What does this mean, and how has it impacted their perspective, bias, and worldview? If over dozens of times and at numerous events in one's childhood these statements were made, would it not have a great impact on perspective and worldview? I would ask participants, "How would this inform your youth, adolescent, and adult perspective?"

All of us have received our values, beliefs, and morals from those closest to us. Our environment certainly plays a role in our worldview. However, I would argue it is those closest to us in our families and extended families that lay the foundation and patterns of justice, fairness, prejudice, tolerance, and intolerance.

If we think about it, the brain is like a file cabinet or a hard drive, a representation of the developing brain, receiving and holding countless files containing the values and beliefs that are given to us by those around us as we are growing up as well as the environmental experiences we have. We are not able to choose and place judgement on these files, as they are given to us at an early age because, developmentally, we have not yet gained the skills of reflection and insight. These developmental skills do not appear for most until around ages eleven or twelve, some not until the early teenage years. If we are constantly fed racist, anti-Semitic, or sexist imagery, subtle or overt, at an early age, those beliefs and values will tend to stay with us until we are able to have insight and begin to create our own self-concept and perspective through our experiences and environment. Many of us who have been given negative imagery and language describing a group of people, other cultures, or religions will carry these opinions and beliefs well into adolescence and adulthood. Sometimes, if we never do the work that I am describing, it will be carried throughout our entire lives.

The other challenge is that some of these biases and negative imagery that we have been given are reinforced over time through the media or real-life experiences in our lives. The fact that racism, sexism, bias toward sexual orientation, gender, and anti-Semitism exist, and exist in such deep and institutionalized ways, makes it very difficult to not become resistant and disillusioned to the potential for change and growth. Many people are simply oblivious to these issues due to gender, class, orientation, and race privilege. The concept of privilege is most commonly connected to affluent white, Christian, heterosexual males, but privilege comes in many forms and can be connected with anyone in a position of power or control. However, understanding and confronting the systemic and embedded systems of racism are challenging for everyone but especially many white people, as they have had the privilege to have lived in a white dominated culture, able to think, act, walk, talk, and function without the need to contemplate or look at another perspective of thinking, not to mention acknowledge their own bias and potential prejudices. Those of other backgrounds, cultures, and races grow up very aware of their "otherness" within a white-dominated society that is wrought with systemic and institutionalized racism.

As W. E. B. Du Bois wrote in *The Souls of Black Folk*, "We are a sort of seventh son, born with a veil, and gifted with second-sight in this American world—a world which yields him no true self-consciousness, but only lets him see himself through the revelation of the other world." Du Bois continues to discuss the concept of double consciousness. He says, "It is a peculiar sensation, this double-consciousness, this sense of always looking at one's self through the eyes of others, of measuring one's soul by the tape of a world that looks on in amused contempt and pity. One ever feels his two-ness—an American, a Negro; two souls, two thoughts, two unreconciled strivings; two warring ideals in one dark body, whose dogged strength alone keeps it from being torn asunder." No one has illuminated this issue more directly and profoundly since Du Bois.

It is the hard work of self-reflection and awareness of one's conscious and unconscious self that begins the process of deleting the files that have been placed in our heads from years of programming by our families, communities, media, and society. I would contend that all people, regardless of race, class, culture, gender, orientation, and position have the need, and I would say personal obligation, to sift through their personal file cabinet and extract those files that they believe are outdated with one's adult sense of self or simply corrupt. Likewise, those values and beliefs that have fortified and strengthened one's experience and resiliency must be investigated and revisited. Even more important than deleting files is the need to continually learn, grow, develop new insight and expand one's understanding of self in relation to the world around them and fortify one's database. We must be willing to continually educate ourselves and learn from our experiences and the world around us. This is a difficult task when we are separated from one another physically, emotionally, and spiritually. Forming an inclusive worldview does not come from attending a class, reading a book, or having a friend in any one of the protected categories. It is a commitment to a daily and lifelong journey and intentionality to elevate one's consciousness and connection to those around us who may be different from ourselves. The irony is once we take the time to explore and learn about the true nature of one another, what is important to us, and what gives us purpose, we will more often than not find that our consciousness is aligned much more closely as Human Beings.

When we are able to look at one another without the filters that we have become accustomed to, the lenses that divide, separate, and categorize and the experiences that have caused deep mistrust, fear, and separation, we can begin to have a deeper connected consciousness, a "soul consciousness" that is founded in love, compassion, peacefulness, nurturing, and spiritual understanding. These values and beliefs transcend anything that divides us. In actuality, they take us right back to the very foundation of our common humanity and purpose. These common values point the way forward for all of us, whether we are aware of them or not, like a soothing voice on a warm and comforting breeze calling us home.

CHAPTER 9

Teh' Ray "Phenom" Hale Sr.

Chicago, Illinois

Both abundance and lack exist simultaneously in our lives, as parallel realities. It is always our conscious choice which secret garden we will tend . . . when we choose not to focus on what is missing from our lives but are grateful for the abundance that's present—love, health, family, friends, work, the joys of nature and personal pursuits that bring us pleasure—the wasteland of illusion falls away and we experience Heaven on earth.
—Sarah Ban Breathnach

I currently work with Phenom on a project focused on outreach to young fathers ages seventeen to twenty-five years old. Phenom is an underground hip-hop artist and youth mentor from Chicago who has spent years working with young adults helping them to find a voice through poetry, art, and self-expression. He was trained by Michelle Obama on the South Side of Chicago with the AmeriCorps program called Public Allies, founded by the Clinton administration in the early '90s. When I met Phenom about eight years ago, it was clear how passionate and experienced he was in his field. When I first heard him perform at an underground hip-hop venue in Hyde Park, his talent as an artist was obvious and powerful, but it was his work around the city combining his artistic skill with youth development work and mentoring that really interested me. Phenom, or Teh' Ray Hale Sr., lives up to his stage name. The relationships that he creates are as authentic as it gets, real, forged through shared experience, dedication, and going the extra mile for those he works with. I see Phenom as an urban sage, sharing wisdom and a deep soulful purpose and connection with people. He calls himself a "Hip-Hop and Youth Development Navy Seal." Whatever it's called, it is some of the most profound, passionate, urban, authentic, artistic youth and young adult work I have come across in my twenty-five-year career. Phenom and I met for this interview at the Fleetwood Jourdain Park District building in Evanston, Illinois, before he was scheduled to meet with his group of young fathers from our mentoring program funded by the Infant Welfare Society of Evanston and the Evanston Community Foundation.

Stephen: Tell me about who you are, where you came from, and the work you do in the community.

Phenom: I was born Teh' Rey Hale and was kind of a gift to the family. The one child who was born in wedlock in my family. My mother had my brother when she was fifteen. The father was in California. Her mother made my mom come back to Chicago to have the baby and alienated the father. So when she was eighteen in Chicago with a three-year-old, her mother forced her hand to marry my father. He was supposedly an upstanding guy in the community, a martial arts instructor, a sensei. He ended up doing security for Imam Wafeen Mohammed. He taught karate to people in the hood. Invited them to his dojo. My father was taking care of my older brother as if he was his, but when I came, my brother kind of felt the shade of having the new baby in the family. I grew up in the Cabrini Green projects.

Stephen: What year was it?

Phenom: It was 1977. I was born in '77. I wasn't really aware of my surroundings till I was four or five years old. In Cabrini, it was the beginning of the crack era and the end of the black power era. Civil Rights was fading out. In Cabrini Green, I saw what I learned later from Elie Wiesel's book *Night* about the Holocaust, how games such as dreidel and others were played while in the hell of the Holocaust. That taught me that inside of a hell-like situation, there can be Heaven. There still can be ways to salvage life, but that's what was happening in Cabrini: violence, poverty, people stacked upon people. Small little shacks on top of one another in a project building. What I realized, though, was everyone I knew was in a two-block radius. My entire world . . . school, grandma, cousins, family, friends, girlfriends, laundromat, grocery store, everything was in this crib, and I had no need to go anywhere. I felt what community was like. Church was there. I got baptized there. Everything happened . . . The news vans came often. There was this huge blacktop between the buildings. Everything happened there. We had to cross the blacktop to get to school. One day, some guys started shooting at the children on the blacktop from one of the buildings and killed one of the kids.

Stephen: While you were walking to school?

Phenom: While we were walking. So that's when I started to begin to learn about the real world. Crazy people. Halloween didn't just have people in masks, but we had rapists and guns. Kids had to go in early. It was lights out when my mom had me in the house. We were latchkey kids. My mom worked at Northwestern Memorial Hospital in the ER. We couldn't call her due to the stressful part of the hospital she was in, so we were on our own most nights.

Stephen: How old were you at this time?

Phenom: It was up until eight or nine years old. We moved out of Cabrini after that.

Stephen: So this was the mid-eighties?

Phenom: Yeah . . . I saw guys shooting guns. I remember seeing the flashes of guns at night. Pow . . . Pow . . . pow. I had an aerial or elevated view of the shootouts from our apartment. It was crazy. The most powerful thing I saw was a guy actually got killed outside of the window. We found out later my mom knew the guy. My uncle knew the guy. It was weird being connected to the situation. The next day on the way to school, there was a pool of blood we had to cross to get to school. This was life. I woke up in this. People would get robbed for food. It was the worst place but, at times also the best place.

Holidays were great. Barbecues, memorial days, the entire community was cooking outside together. It was amazing. Christmas, birthdays everyone was there. This is what set my meter on how good life can be and how bad it can be. As I grew, I could see who was faking violence. I knew when real violence was coming. Wannabe gangbangers, tough guys in stores trying to act tough. Being aware of what it is and isn't.

We moved out of Cabrini Green in the mid-eighties to the West Town neighborhood of Chicago. This was the first time I met a Mexican person or smelled Mexican food in a friend's house. My first best friend was a white kid named Matthew Mika. People used to tease him about missing a finger on one of his hands, and I wanted to defend him. It wasn't his fault. I think it got cut off in a washing machine.

Stephen: Sounds like the beginning of your social justice work?

Phenom: Yeah. I wanted to defend him from that. He was a cool dude. I went over to his house and met his family. He had a three-level house and an intercom. I was exposed to family at the dinner table. I saw what family was supposed to be like. I felt special just being over there.

Stephen: So you were invited into their house like a part of the family?

Phenom: Definitely. They loved me, and I loved them. I had a lot of energy in those days. I got kicked out of school in seventh grade. I was active. School was boring to me. It was just boring. I had drug dealers in my house and people shooting around me. Guns were hidden in my house. I had drugs chopped up in my house. It was behind the scenes of what was happening in Grandma's house.

Stephen: I have to go back because you had said your mom had married your father who was an upstanding guy . . . Where was he? Did he leave early on?

Phenom: Yes, they lasted . . . I'm not exactly sure how long, but by the time I was four or five, he was no longer in the picture. I remember seeing him when I was about five at my grandma's house. He picked me up, so I knew I was little. He had a Nutter Butter candy bar in his shirt pocket. I said, "What's that?"

He said, "That's for you." That was the first and last thing I remember receiving from my father. I took it, and I don't remember seeing him after that.

Stephen: So with all that you shared growing up, a lot of deep stuff, violence, and struggle, where was the change in you or the click that made you want to give back and help people?

Phenom: I think it was a progression of things, but I remember one of my teachers, Ms. Hodges, gave me a poem to read in front of class.

Stephen: What was it?

Phenom: Clarence Darrow's "Reach for Your Dream." It was a speech! That's what it was—a speech. I read it out loud, and they loved it. I got applause. It was the first time.

Stephen: How old were you?

Phenom: I don't know, maybe eight or nine. She said that I was going to be in the assembly the next week. It was a big deal. I killed it. Everyone was happy. I got a lot of praise. So they said they were going to put me in the regional contest. An oratory contest. I was able to be out of school. I was performing in front of people. They took me to McDonald's. This was great for a nine-year-old. I felt great. I felt something special about doing something special. I was at Kennedy-King College. It was the first time I had ever been in a college. I got fourth place, and I was pissed off. I thought I was better and wanted to win it. I went home and cried, but that was the first time I realized I had a talent. A little later, we moved West and then to Oak Park, and I went to Julian Middle School. That was where I wrote my first rhyme.

Stephen: This was around 1987, 1988?

Phenom: Yes . . . Hip-hop was out. LL Cool J . . . my brothers and uncles fell in love with hip-hop and so did I. My first rhyme I said in public was in the boy's locker room, and it was a hit. They kept asking me to say it over and over. I decided I needed to write more rhymes. By that time, I went to Oak Park River Forest High School and met Darrien Sutton. He was rhyming already, and we started a crew. We were called Phamily Jewels. I changed my stage name from Succotash to Phenom. We were actually signed by this guy E-Smooth with visionary records. He also had Kanye West on his label.

Stephen: So you met Kanye when you were seventeen or eighteen?

Phenom: Absolutely. I think we were not commercial enough for E-Smooth. We all did a show together at the Double Door that year in

Chicago. Kanye eventually moved on and went to New York. This was about the time I joined Public Allies.

Stephen: You joined Public Allies while you were still in high school?

Phenom: I was eighteen . . . the moment I graduated from high school. Public Allies is a community service program run by AmeriCorps.

Stephen: Where did you hear about it?

Phenom: I heard about it through a community job I had in the hood. There was a community center called Emerson House in the West Town community. I became a summer program counselor, like a youth outreach worker. I wanted to be active and really wanted to work with the kids. I started a summer basketball league at this community center.

Stephen: So I have to pause a second and ask a question . . . You are in your thirties now, have been doing great work with young people for many years, but you just told me your story about growing up in Cabrini Green and dealing with a lot of violence, pain, and other issues. At age seventeen, you started giving back and doing positive stuff in the West Town community of Chicago. Not everyone does that at that age. In actuality, a lot of sixteen- and seventeen-years-old's who grew up in tough circumstances are getting into more trouble. How did you already have a consciousness about being positive at that age?

Phenom: Our house growing up was open . . . We had friends of the family in the house all the time. My grandmother was a community-focused person. She would help people out by letting them stay with us. I had to learn how to adjust to different people. They called my grandmother "sister." That was her name in the community.

Stephen: It sounds like your grandma was a critical person . . . Tell me more about Public Allies and the experience you got with them.

Phenom: When I was running this program at Emerson House, one of the supervisors said I should apply for Public Allies. They gave me the application. I wrote an essay on cleaning up the community and cleaning our parks to make the space better for youth. So they got the essay and called me for an interview. The first person I saw was Michelle Obama. She was a young director at Public Allies. They hired forty of us to be community change agents. They split us in four different groups. Each group had an issue to address in the community: public health, education, economics, and a faith-based group. We had ten people in each group and had to find a board or steering committee. I was learning about boards, communities of Chicago, gentrification, and all these different things and would try to bring this information back to the hood, and people would not know what I was talking about. I was getting an education. They exposed me to all these things and, in ten months, gave me $5,000 for college. I was making $500 every two weeks at age nineteen. I was doing well. I got my own apartment. I was feeling great. Going to school, had a job. It was going so well I thought it was good enough to have a baby. I had my first child at twenty-one. At age twenty-two, I felt like I had a lot to teach. Michelle Obama plugged me into Mt. Sinai Hospital. I was bringing kids in through a community outreach program working with kids from the community.

Stephen: Were you doing music the whole time you were doing the Public Allies track?

Phenom: Yes . . . at the very same time and incorporating it into the work. I won an award from Mayor Daley and Superintendent Hillard for running the top youth program in the city. At the same time, I had just had my son. I broke up with my crew. Some of my guys went to Atlanta. Ludacris, who was at our school earlier on, went to Atlanta.

Stephen: I didn't know Ludacris was from Chicago.

Phenom: Ludacris was from here, Chi City! This is where he learned how to rhyme.

Stephen: He never says anything about Chicago.

Phenom: That was our problem with him.

Stephen: Kanye always talks about Chicago. Common talks about Chicago.

Phenom: Absolutely. Absolutely. I guess Atlanta showed him a lot of love, and that's where he really got "put on." So that's where he shows love.

Stephen: So outside of the hip-hop stuff, you had this Public Allies thing, this community service thing. I'm sure you had ambition in the hip-hop world, but you also had something else driving you. You hear it in your music now and the messages you give. I'm talking on a spiritual level. When you give back and care about people coming up behind you, there is something else going on besides your own ambition. Not everyone winds up being like that, especially in the hip-hop world.

Phenom: My family loved me well. Not with material things. I didn't have a lot of toys and stuff, but I appreciated people in my family like my uncle James. So I learned a lot from family. I learned a lot from even gang leaders . . . They showed love. My mother took us to church religiously. At church . . . it was True Rock Pentecostal Church. Pastor Earl Granberry. He loved on those people, and what stood out to me the most was the annual church picnic. I felt so good on those days. I had no idea what time it was, where we were. It turned out it was behind McCormick place on the lake. That's where our church had its picnic. That's where I felt love and beauty. It was a positive environment.

Stephen: It sounds like the faith and religious connections were profound to you, but a contradiction from the violence you saw and felt in the Cabrini community you grew up in?

Phenom: It was prime opportunity to love someone out of their funk. That's what was happening at church. You didn't get turned away from doing bad. You got loved on harder but holding someone accountable. Coming home and loving the good parts of someone who was doing bad makes them want to do good. Love is good. It was a platform for me coming home.

Stephen: Working with families, youth, and young adults as you do, do you feel spirituality plays a big role in your work and how you operate?

Phenom: It's like the basic construct, the foundation of the world I live in. From rhyming to teaching to chilling with some of the guys in the fatherhood program. There is a spiritual accountability that I hold myself to. I know that I don't want to feel a certain way when I reflect on my day. I don't want to feel the conviction of others, so I am proactive for guiding myself.

Stephen: The heart of this book is about people but also about spirituality. Do you believe in a soul, and what does that look like to you?

Phenom: Absolutely. A soul is the basic core of being. A soul dives out in the street to save that baby. It's spirit. A natural reaction. But souls can also be good and bad. The human piece of it is what directs it. The soul helps me to understand that it's really the basic building block of what God uses for everyone.

Stephen: Even the people who were committing the violence you were talking about earlier?

Phenom: Yes. Those people have a soul, but I learned from Public Allies that hurt people hurt people. There are killers out here.

Stephen: Are people like that blind to their own soul?

Phenom: I would like to say that something is missing, and they are incomplete, but what I did learn through the rap game and my political education is how the forces outside of us can exacerbate the soul. Knowing that, I am constantly looking for the platform to talk to that soul or turn that person's soul. I try to talk to people who are killing out here, that they may have an issue with someone or a gang member, but I tell them they're also killing their girlfriend and their unborn baby when they shoot. There are innocents out here too, and they are being killed by those stray bullets.

Stephen: That brings up the black-on-black violence issue, even the violence with the police we have been seeing around the country and the Black Lives Matter movement. How does that fit into all this?

Phenom: It's an imbalance of power . . . of belonging . . . an imbalance of a bunch of things that's missing. Let's talk externally first. Steve, the world we live in is tipped. It's tipped for us to hate ourselves. It's loaded. As a rapper or emcee, if I got on wax and said, "I'm killing so and so or a specific group of people," there are going to be repercussions in that community. Whatever groups we would be dissing our words would be looked down upon and seen as unacceptable, but we can say we can kill ourselves or kill "these niggas" and get a fat-ass check.

Stephen: Meaning the system, or music industry, promotes violence?

Phenom: There is not another race where it is promoted like that.

Stephen: For black people to commit crime against other black people?

Phenom: Absolutely. Even on Eminem's tape when he was getting famous . . . he did a skit where he said that he was not making any money, and the record executive says, "Well, Dr. Dre is talking about blunts, 40s, niggers, and bitches." What are you talking about? He was hinting that there is a formula to the success. That is in us, man, and we know it.

Stephen: But isn't that what creates the underground movement, which you are a part of and a leader of the underground hip-hop movement in Chicago.

Phenom: Absolutely, man, there is an imbalance with that. We stick to try to even that imbalance. So that's one thing . . . The system is loaded. Two. Let's look at the Black Lives Matter movement. It was originally the red flag and the blue flag coming together against the police flag.

Stephen: You mean Crips and Bloods?

Phenom: That was a togetherness, a unity and truce, inside of a violent community that had the scales tipped against them. So there is unity inside of that situation. There were blacks who were not a part of the gang world and came to the meetings and barbecues and decided to tweet and hashtag, and they are the ones who got the attention.

Stephen: You mean it became more political?

Phenom: It kind of changed the unity that was created, the original people that came together in those gang truces sort of got co-opted for political purposes. Now let's look at some of these events where Black Lives Matter has gotten involved. The system has created an environment . . . where a man can tell an officer he has a legal weapon in the car, calmly go for his ID, and still get shot. Then you have a man walking toward a car with his hands up. Yes, he wasn't obeying orders, but his arms are up. Then he's shot. Police aren't taught about a de-escalation process, but there are a few other things that baffle me. That guy Dylan Roof, who killed nine people. When the police got to the scene, he had a gun on him, just killed nine people, and he walks away in custody of the police. This guy told you he had a gun, and you killed him. This other guy had his hands up, and you kill him. Dylan Roof murders nine people and walks away from the scene in custody. Nine people.

Stephen: A double standard.

Phenom: Steve, they just got a kid in a school who killed a bunch of people with an automatic weapon in his hands. He is in custody. It's tipped, Steve, but that makes us right there hate ourselves. It's okay for us to die. Look, we are considered to be roaches and rats. As opposed to snakes. Snakes are vicious, way more than a rat or roach, but the roaches get sprayed or stomped upon on site. Rats are baited with traps and snapped in the worst way. Snakes are hunted, captured, and taken away somewhere. Released in the wild or brought to a shelter. Snakes can eat your baby. They are far more dangerous. That is the same conditioning for black folks in this place.

Stephen: Man, a bunch of questions just popped in my head. So one thing that comes to mind is that we know we live in a world where there are hundreds of years of inequality and racist imagery that has been promoted. We know the police department is part of that system, so officers have the same bias and prejudice, and it's brought out in a split-second situation. How do we change this beyond training use of nonlethal force because that person came up in a world of bias and prejudice . . . How do we change that?

Phenom: There are many issues that need to be changed. We need to find out the place to start. That's why I am where I am. You start with the youth. You kind of catch the seeds that were planted, but there is going to have to be a continual system of showing youth the positives out there.

Stephen: What would you say most of the youth you work with around Chicago . . . What is the general perception and feeling about cops?

Phenom: It's to hate cops. If you don't, then you are in trouble with the community.

Stephen: That's a tough thing to unwind.

Phenom: If you start training to be a cop or choose to join the force, you have automatically chosen a side that is not aligned with the community.

Stephen: I know this is complicated, but is part of the answer finding more people from the neighborhood to be cops, to care about their community, to look like their community, to walk in their community, to know their community?

Phenom: I have this petri dish that I call the Lyric Lagoon. It's a lab where I can test theories on how to make things work. Out of eight years of running this thing, I have not had one fight.

Stephen: Is this in Hyde Park?

Phenom: No, this was terror town, Seventy-Ninth and Jeffery, Southeast Side. This is a place that is forgotten about. That's where we started. We were there for a few years. This was a culmination of everything I had learned about how to work with youth and the community. A cocktail of what worked and extracting of what didn't work. The youth came up with the name. This was out of South Shore High School. Once they came up with a name, they gave it identity, then we held them to a standard for that identity. We created this environment of love, peace . . . It was temporary or haphazard, but it was there. You would get a form of a mother, father, sister, or brother. A form of dinner together, accountability, a check-in. Hey, how was school today? What happened with . . . ? These were kids who were homeless or ran away or had breakdowns. In there were cops and preachers, but they were not called that. They just did the work. It draws these people into the open mics we did. It was just an environment we created. There are great cops. . . great people from the community, but when they put on that blue shirt, it sets people off. It reminds us of . . . the same way a lady grabs her purse when a black man walks by or locking the door when a group of people walk by.

Stephen: It's almost like trauma. People have been traumatized.

Phenom: The way to do it is to get the youth and put them in this environment . . . it's been working. Kids come in getting praise about their new job. They have a place to go and tell someone about their life.

Stephen: So here is the million-dollar question . . . I agree with you about this as a part of the solution, but are there enough Phenoms or Lyric Lagoons to stem the tide of what we see happening? There is so much murder and shooting going on . . . Another weekend and there are seventeen more murders and thirty-five people shot in Chicago. How do you change the narrative?

Phenom: I lived a while and never thought I would see peace in certain areas. It was so bad in some places I came up in, but I have seen change. There has to be some anger in our community about what's going on.

When you are not angry, you just tend to accept it. When you get angry, you are forced to change some shit. We are angry, but we're not angry enough. There are a finite amount of blocks, Steve. We can chop them up and be there when the situation comes up as opposed to being there post situation.

Stephen: I have one last question for you . . . It makes me think of resiliency. People have always done this. Keep fighting in the work we do. The question is how do you personally stay resilient? What makes you stay positive in the fight and keeps you going?

Phenom: One, I would say my upbringing. Things I was taught by family and friends, but once I go past that, I would say Michelle Obama gave me this great visual. We did a trust fall, but it was in a circle where you fall in any direction and have to get pushed back up to the center. We were taught how important it was to put people like that around in your circle. So that when you do fall, you fall on someone you can trust, and that is trustworthy enough to push you back up. The focus then became building the circle around you.

Stephen: That's deep.

Phenom: There are youth who are pillars. They are strong and resilient. They can go through fire and water. They are excellent kids. You just have to dust off those blocks they have around their soul, and they will shine for you in your darkness. With people such as yourself, Roberto, Pastor Phil, Enoch Muhammed, Joseph, E-way . . . putting those people around you helps when you start to wobble. Out of nowhere, they inflate you . . . push you back to center. Man, that makes me feel great. When I can make an impact on a kid and they start shining or they leave a program glowing, it makes me feel like I'm glowing. If I'm shining and I don't have anyone blocking my shine or my soul, it passes on. Where did you get that shine from? It's inside of us, and it comes from helping others. When I feel great, others feel great, and you're in a system that elevates everyone. There will always be something that tests the resiliency of that circle, and that's the process. Continuing to fortify the circle, by each brick, dusting off the soul, man, so that it can be strong enough to withstand any pressure.

CHAPTER 10

Voices of a Nation

The land flourished because it was fed from so many sources—because it was nourished by so many cultures and traditions and peoples.
—Lyndon B. Johnson

I was fortunate to be able to take a small vacation and drive from Chicago to Washington DC with my wife and three young children to the presidential inauguration of Barack Obama in 2008. It was an incredible experience to be a part of a movement that focused on hope, change, and the promise of transformation with the election of the first African American president in our nation's history. We were five of almost two million people that descended upon the DC area that day. It was a madhouse of people, traffic, and blocked-off streets, but it was incredibly positive and moving to be part of a sea of onlookers, feeling a common sense of optimism and belief in the future of our country and its ability to be better than its past. Change had come to the United States, whether Democrat, Republican, or independent. The reality of embarking on a new era was undeniable, at least, so we thought. Unfortunately, the following years of congressional gridlock and personal and political agendas left much to be desired.

One of the constants in our imperfect union that was fought for by our founding fathers and their activist descendants has been the right to protest, speak out, demand justice, and codify change through our constitutional rights. We have the directed ability to make changes and amendments to our constitution and laws, which govern our people. The very fact that our founders allowed for amendments with a special vote in congress was because they had the foresight to realize that change in an enduring institution or nation was inevitable, even as many were slave owners and part of a fundamentally oppressive and deeply unequal system themselves. We have seen numerous debates, movements, acts, changes, and amendments to the constitution and our government over the years—Roosevelt's New Deal that was created over a span of eight years in a response to the Great Depression in the 1930s, the Civil Rights Act of 1968, the Equal Rights Amendment of 1972, and the Supreme Court voting to uphold gay marriage as a national right in 2015. Change is a constant. Our ability as a people to manage, react, guide, and respond to the desire for change through conversations, debate, and peaceful protest in open and public forums is the critical challenge we face and an obligation as Americans. Much of this challenge and ongoing fracture in our society is due to deep historical divides of our people that can be traced back to before the Civil War, before slavery to the very beginnings of colonialism and European expansionism. The legacy of oppression and marginalization of people runs long and deep in our country. It is the underside of our democratic and capitalistic experiment, which, for many groups of people, has been an exclusionary experience creating deep chasms of distrust, pain, resentment, even death and genocide. Others in our society have benefited from a system of privilege and power, which has been systematically created to support and assist in maintaining that power, privilege, and existence of a white, male, Judeo-Christian, and cisgender cultural hierarchy. While economic divides have grown more profound and the middle class has shrunk dramatically in our country over the last forty years, making the American dream even more distant for poor white folks as well, the racial, cultural, and ethnic chasm that exists between our people, regardless of economic status, is profound.

On June 17, 2015, we endured yet another racially motivated hate crime in Charleston, South Carolina. Nine black Americans were shot in cold blood while at a Bible study at the Emmanuel African Methodist Episcopal (AME) Church, which was the scene of this horrific crime. We found out quickly that the shooter, Dylan Roof, age twenty-one, was a supporter of the Southern Confederacy, white supremacy groups, and apartheid-era South Africa and Rhodesia, which was ruled by a white minority until 1980, when it became Zimbabwe.

Nine cold-blooded murders shook the nation. Republican governors across the South began debating the removal of the Confederate flag from public institutions and place them in museums where many believed they belonged for a long time. There would be a backlash from some. Some states were less willing to remove the Confederate flag and symbols of the Confederacy from public spaces and their capital . . . mostly those who follow white supremacy groups, the Ku Klux Klan, skinhead groups, the Southern Confederacy, and white folks who may not be affiliated with these groups but feel threatened by a growing non-white majority in our national population. Those who say it is a symbol of their heritage and Southern pride were ready for confrontation. In some states, there were clashes and protests on both sides, setting up a more violent and confrontational situation.

In Baltimore, Maryland, and Ferguson, Missouri, a few months earlier in 2015, we saw protests, street violence, and rioting in response to conspicuous deaths and potential murders of black citizens by the hands of the police. A storm of protests, peaceful gatherings, and angry marches across the country erupted with the rallying cry of "Black Lives Matter."

A few months later, a woman from Chicago, Sandra Bland, was pulled over in her car in Waller County, Texas, on July 13, 2015. The cause of her arrest is questionable at best. Her three nights in a jail cell and reported suicide by hanging with twisted-up plastic bags is even more suspect. Another death, more questions, and black communities and concerned people across the country take a deep breath as another human being dies in the custody of the police.

The nonstop occurrence of these incidents of police abuse of power, lethal force, and, in some cases, murder have been exhausting and unbearable. The systemic and institutionalized racism that exists within the police department and Department of Justice, coupled with the hopelessness and helplessness felt by many who have been disenfranchised and locked out of opportunity has created a powder keg ready to explode. The discussion of police brutality within the black community, the need for better relationships between our police departments and urban communities as well as urban violence, gun control, black-on-black crime, and the Second Amendment would be ongoing issues of controversy and discussion among many Americans throughout 2015, 2016, 2017, and beyond. Though these incidents have been happening for years, the introduction of cell phone technology and social media has changed the visual impact and brought these issue to national attention.

I was downtown shopping with my family in Chicago a few weeks after the release of the Laquan McDonald video, which showed, once again, a young black man being shot by a Chicago police officer sixteen times on the South Side. Protests for the Black Lives Matter movement and others in the activist community in Chicago had been going on for weeks, demanding justice. They were calling for the resignation of Mayor Rahm Emanuel and the Illinois State's attorney, Anita Alvarez, specifically because the tape was held for so long and only released after being pushed by local media outlets. It screamed of a cover-up during the Chicago mayoral election of Rahm Emanuel versus Jesus "Chuy" Garcia, who could have been the first Latino mayor of Chicago, ten months earlier.

About three hundred or so protesters made their way down Michigan Avenue. We heard chanting and saw signs in the distance. As they got closer, I asked all three of my children to come over to me. They were ages fifteen, thirteen, and ten at the time. I told them that we were going to join the protest and not simply watch them go by us. They were initially surprised, but we had all been watching the events unfold on the news. My children, who attend CPS schools, lived in Chicago all their lives and grew up in Logan Square and Austin on the West Side, are very aware of the issues around us in the community related to police misconduct and violence against people of color. They understood very clearly why people were so upset. We stepped off the sidewalk and into the crowd of protesters, and we quickly joined in the energy and excitement of the group. This was a peaceful protest, but the anger and frustration were palpable. People were chanting "Sixteen shots and a cover up" and "Rahm Emmanuel, it's time to go." "Anita Alvarez, you moved too slow." We all joined in the rhythm and energy of the crowd. We cleared both lanes of the Magnificent Mile, the largest economic engine in the city of Chicago and a prestigious and high-class shopping district, with stores such as Cartier, Bloomingdales, and Crate and Barrel. This was also the Christmas shopping season. Hundreds of tourists and holiday shoppers were out spending their money. Black Lives Matter and the protesters were clearly making their point that "business as usual" cannot go on.

The police were there in force, most on bikes, flanking the protesters, using their bikes as barriers. I thought to myself that this was a very smart play by the police. They were nonconfrontational but clearly given orders to use their bikes and large numbers to direct our movements. Many of the police were very calm and friendly, the younger officers appeared nervous and looking for direction from their superior. The police did a good job of respecting and at the same time controlling the crowd, which now included myself and my three children. At one point, however, the leadership of the protesters made a quick directional change and lead the group off Michigan Avenue and down the opposite way of a one-way street that fed into the "Magnificent Mile." The police were clearly not ready or prepared for this move. The bike cops all started moving quickly and looking for direction, but they could not anticipate the moves of the crowd and all the sudden chaos seemed to break out. Protesters were head on with traffic, walking around cars, on the sidewalks, chanting and moving quickly. The crowd of protesters, including myself, began running and moving more quickly through the city street just west of Michigan Avenue, where the protest had begun. The police were clearly not ready for this move as they may have assumed the protest would be confined to the shopping district. Most people made their way back to Michigan Avenue after about ten minutes, but the crowd of two hundred to three hundred people at this point were clearly in control of this three-block downtown area. Soon after, we were being corralled back to our protest area, and the police became more agitated, and some arguments broke out. There was an attempt to push the protesters to a single side of the street and allow traffic to flow again. Clearly, the police were trying to assert their authority. As tensions started to rise and a few hot spots seemed to be moving toward arrests, I decided it was time to lead my three children back to the sidewalk and away from any potential violence.

I think my children understood what we were doing and why. I think the energy and adrenalin of being in their first protest or march for a cause that had purpose and meaning for them was a powerful lesson. They had a voice. They can stand up for what they believe in. There is the right to freedom of speech and assembly in our country, to peacefully voice your opinion and fight against the systems of inequality that exist.

The next day, another unarmed black man was killed by a white officer in another city, in some other part of the United States. His wife and child were in the car and watched him die as four bullets went into his chest. It was streamed on Facebook for all to see.

Social media and smartphones have changed how these incidents are seen and experienced. They are in your face, at the moment, and the documentation in real time is powerful. It was posted and reposted. Played over and over on local and national news media. It illuminates and broadcasts what has been taking place for many, many years with police brutality in the black and brown community and, more specifically, with black men and boys. At the same time, the public is using these videos, body cameras, and police video can just as easily prove warranted police actions in the face of illegal and criminal behavior as well as police misconduct and abuses. Either way, it is a powder keg of visual and visceral information that the media injects every night into the American conversation and psyche.

We need honest accounts of the abuses and criminality taking place in our communities, but we also need honest accounts of the breadth and diversity of our communities and the activities that we are engaged in. That they are not all violent. That all police are not abusing power. That all black men are not criminals. That people are engaged in positive change efforts around the country. That goodness, compassion, empathy, and caring still exists. Fathers are raising their children. People are still playing in the parks without incident. People of different races and backgrounds do get together. Programs and positive activities are in action trying to counter what is taking place in Chicago and other cities around the country.

I understand that these incidents of violence must be covered by the media. Justice is a right as is freedom of the press. It would be nice, however, if the media also covered some of the more positive messages on their evening broadcast as well. Unfortunately, it just doesn't get the airplay and ratings their sponsors need. Violence, unrest, and police confrontation sells and sells well.

The underlying issues that create the opportunity for police brutality and excessive force are deeper than a need for improved training and enhanced community policing can solve. Though the issues of training around excessive force must be discussed and access to tasers and other nonlethal means to peacefully de-escalate situations must be implemented for all officers, there is a narrative in our country that many seem do not want to address and discuss.

Our nation has perpetuated and reinforced hundreds of years of negative imagery and stereotypes of black and brown people. We have lived mostly isolated from one another. The systems of inequality that have been created over these hundreds of years have increased economic disparity, encouraged cultural isolation, and limited our ability to really know one another beyond the stereotypes and generalizations fed to us by the media. We do not know one another as a people. Of course, there are some of us that have built multicultural friendships and relationships; but for a vast majority of people in the United States, this is not the case. We have embedded bias and stereotypes in our subconscious, which feed our fear and feelings of otherness. Why does a white woman clutch her purse in an elevator when a black man walks in? Why does a security attendant follow a person of color in a department store and not the white person that walked in behind them? Why does the landlord not rent to the Latino mother and children but will bend over backward to rent to a white woman with the same number of children? Why does a white student in a college setting get probation or community service for violent sexual assault while a black person will get ten to twelve years in prison?

These questions refer to a deeper discussion that must be had. An ownership of our collective historical narrative in this country. A history of structural oppression, institutionalized segregation, systemic racism, economic inequality, and lack of opportunity, conscious and unconscious bias, stereotyping, and perpetuation of historical myths and manipulation of our shared identity as human beings. It is time for a reckoning, fellow Americans, with our deepest and darkest thoughts, our conscious and/or unconscious mind that guide our behaviors and actions, forms our values, and belief systems and makes us act out on our worst fears. We must own our American history of inequity, all of us, and the role we have played, both consciously and unconsciously in its unfortunate perpetuation.

Chapter 11

Anndrea Miller

Chicago, Illinois

Our deepest fear is not that we are inadequate. Our deepest fear is that we are powerful beyond measure. It is our light, not our darkness, that most frightens us. We ask ourselves, who am I to be brilliant, gorgeous, talented and fabulous? Actually, who are you not to be? You are a child of God. Your playing small does not serve the world. There is nothing enlightened about shrinking so that other people won't feel insecure around you. We are born to make manifest the Glory of God that is within us. It is not just in some of us, it's in everyone. And as we let our own light shine, we unconsciously give other people permission to do the same. As we are liberated from our own fear, our presence automatically liberates others.
— Marianne Williamson

I met Anndrea Miller four years ago as an executive director with the YMCA of Metropolitan Chicago. At the time of this interview, she was running the Rauner branch of the YMCA in the South Side neighborhood of Pilsen/Little Village. She is a leader of great passion and cultural insight. Anndrea is a strong advocate of community and values communication, inclusion, and dialogue. She is vocal, opinionated, and constantly questions herself and those around her to elevate conversations about those she serves. We met on a Thursday evening after Anndrea had been hosting a staff BBQ and gathering. This is a great example of her commitment to her leadership team, her employees, and the people they serve. Her commitment to community is profound.

She picked a local taqueria on Western Avenue to meet and record this interview over some cold Negra Modelo's and enchiladas suizas. The location was a small authentic Mexican restaurant down the street from her YMCA center. The authenticity and character of this local Chicago restaurant was a perfect reflection of community, culture, and ethnic cuisine. It was a pleasure to sit with my good friend and hear her story.

Stephen: Tell me about who you are, your background, and what you do.

Anndrea: That is a forever evolving process. I was originally born and raised in Columbus, Ohio. I am a Buckeye through and through. What I do currently, I am a bridge builder within communities. My official title says executive director, but I find myself out meeting people and greeting people. Trying to find ways to welcome people. I am a big sister of many. I have sixteen siblings.

Stephen: How many?

Anndrea: Sixteen. I may have to recount, but—

Stephen: We could do a whole book on that. Tell me about that.

Anndrea: It's a very interesting story. It was definitely one of those poppa-was-a-rolling-stone stories. But yeah . . . two of my siblings I grew up with. The others I met and connected with over time. Recently, we found out we have another sibling we came to be aware of. She is in Arizona, and we're trying to figure out how we can connect.

Stephen: Where do you fall in the order?

Anndrea: I am the oldest.

Stephen: That's an interesting role to play.

Anndrea: I'm the oldest, so to some degree, I feel responsible and want us all somehow to connect and get together.

Stephen: Did you know your dad when you were younger?

Anndrea: I met him when I was sixteen. We knew of each other, but to have an actual interaction with him, I was sixteen.

Stephen: So did you grow up and spend most of your life in Ohio?

Anndrea: Yeah, Columbus. Born and raised went to high school and college. Never left until I came to Chicago. It's a family town. A foodie town. There are a lot of people that come through Columbus. It was voted the smartest city . . . Not sure what that means.

Stephen: It's better than being known for the most homicides.

Anndrea: Hello. It's a good place. It has its challenges like everywhere, but it's a good place. There are a lot of things people don't understand. It's a good place. I like to believe I am person that is inspirational and gives people some light. So I try to share and inspire, even if it's about Columbus.

Stephen: You said before when you mentioned your dad that you felt some responsibility as the oldest sibling. Tell me about that.

Anndrea: The interesting thing is that he has played a huge role in connecting us. That we know who we are and that we are related. For him, I think he was really young and didn't get the magnitude of what being present was. As he's gotten older, I think you learn the power of interpersonal relationships, the power of human connection, what that feels like, and you want to get involved. I have siblings that live in Chicago, and they are young, like eleven and eight. He's got these two sets. We refer to first set and second set. It's interesting. The more I get to know about him, the more I learn about myself. It's cliché but true. I see myself in my mom, but to see myself in him is really intriguing.

Stephen: I know you are here in Chicago now and are the executive director at the YMCA. Can you tell me about your experience and what you do at the YMCA?

Anndrea: There are so many things that you do as an executive director. But this Y is different for me because, for one, I don't reflect the demographic of the community the Y sits in. So the last few years has been me beginning to understand where I am, learning about some of the needs the community has, learning about the culture. How disconnected the Y is and ways the Y could be better connected but, more importantly, to figure out how the Y can become a part of the community instead of always looking at it with the standpoint of the community becoming a part of the YMCA.

Stephen: Can you explain what you mean by the culture and why you aren't a part of the culture. What are the demographics?

Anndrea: Our demographic is Hispanic/Latino, but my staff will tell you in a heartbeat that it's Mexican. The Pilsen/Little Village community is probably 85 percent Mexican. I personally am from an African American/black community, and so it's different. I don't speak Spanish—*estoy aprendiendo el Español*—but it's coming slower than I thought it would. Just understanding the black and brown relations that are happening. Being naïve in a sense and thinking we are all people of color so we all have the same struggles, we don't. There are definitely differences.

Stephen: What are some of the black and brown relations that you have seen?

Anndrea: I've seen there is mistrust and distrust. There is some curiosity. I've seen that there is . . . at times, a desire to want to connect but just lack of awareness and education on how. To be able to make that happen. I see that there has been a long-standing history and depending on what demographic you are dealing with as it relates to black and brown it may be different. There is some acceptance, and then there is lack of acceptance. A lot of that is like most human conflicts, misunderstanding, and ignorance. Not ignorance in the sense of incompetence, but ignorance of truly fearing the unknown.

Stephen: Fearing of other?

Anndrea: Yes.

Stephen: You had mentioned that the two years you have been here has been figuring all this out, building bridges. Have you figured it out? Have there been some positives and negatives? Can you share some of that?

Anndrea: I think there has been both. When you are building trust, you know it's like how the saying goes: "It takes forever to build and seconds to destroy." I am constantly walking a fine line to make sure I don't fall out of the graces with the people I have been able to cultivate relationships with. You know, we get comment cards, and I have noticed more people saying, "I've noticed there are a lot more black people coming to the Y." It goes downhill from there. You know, people saying, "We should keep the Y the way it is."

Stephen: You mean keep it Mexican?

Anndrea: Yes.

Stephen: How do you respond to something like that? As a black person and then as an executive director?

Anndrea: First, you have to digest it and not take it personally. When I first got this comment card, I don't think I was in a space to not take it personally but to understand where that person was coming from and see it through their lens and to understand that you are working with a culture and community that is used to having things taken from them, used to have people making decisions for them, whether it is a language barrier or culture or whatever. I get it now. Back then, I wanted to explain it and try to have people understand that the city is diverse, the neighborhood is changing, etc.

I still believe we need to be as inclusive as we possibly can, but I think that it is important that in order to be inclusive does not mean to exclude those that have already belonged. That's the piece I think that gets lost. Us trying to be so inclusive, we sometimes forget about those that have been here and paved the way for the reason this place exists, whether it's the Y or any other community organization.

Stephen: Did you have a pretty big learning curve about the Mexican community, the Chicago Mexican community, what that meant, what it didn't?

Anndrea: I think so, I don't know if I still don't know.

Stephen: You are still on that curve?

Anndrea: I think I'm in my parabola and still on my way up.

Stephen: Sometimes it just keeps going.

Anndrea: Yeah, for sure, but it's a lot more enjoyable now. The growing pains don't feel as painful.

Stephen: So my next question is along these lines: what sustains you in this work and keeps you motivated?

Anndrea: The fact that I can feel the growth. I can't quantify it, but I can feel the change. I can see it in the people, the work. It just feels completely different. The way people respond to one another, respond to me. The staff, members, community. All of the above. I have recently been invited to several community meetings that I didn't even know existed a year ago. All from having a simple conversation with someone. Them trusting me enough to introduce me to someone else, and now we are connected.

Stephen: Question . . . on that piece. I totally get that as a person of a different culture, you have to build trust, especially in Chicago, because there is such a lack of trust between cultures.

Anndrea: This is by far the most shocking thing for me. Chicago, at a quick glance, you notice how racially segregated it is, but when you take a deeper look, there is social segregation that happens as well.

Stephen: What I was going to ask was do you feel you have been invited to these events now because people have overcome this fear of other or because you specifically have certain intrinsic qualities that build bridges?

Anndrea: My gut tells me that it may be more of the first, and I hope it doesn't have much to do with me.

Stephen: Why do you say that?

Anndrea: Because I think that there is only so much one person can do. It's really more about the collective of the group and what's best for that group as opposed to the individual.

Stephen: Do you think you brought vision to this center?

Anndrea: I think now we have some vision, and if it's not vision just yet, there is at least direction.

Stephen: That's part of what feeds you right? That you have gone down the road a bit?

Anndrea: Yes, for sure . . . the evolution of progress.

Stephen: That's a good thing in the work we do . . . validation.

Anndrea: It is. And it feels good. It feels good to see someone else feel good. That in itself can sustain and motivate you.

Stephen: Let me ask this question . . . How does faith play a role in your community and the work you do personally? You can take the word "faith" in any way you want.

Anndrea: Faith in the community is . . . there is a lot of tradition and as it relates to faith and religion. Those things are correlated very strongly in this community. For me, I think faith is part of internal belief and part of external systems, i.e., religion, spirituality that is learned from outside sources. I think your ability to believe in something is faith. Someone has a belief or something they are strongly moved by or want to pursue—and it's not black and white like most things—and be able to approach the unknown to navigate that, that's faith. You need it.

Stephen: What about you personally?

Anndrea: I believe that there are things that happen in the universe that are predestined. I believe there are things that happen in the universe that we create. I believe faith intersects both of those.

Stephen: Has that fortified you and your belief system and the work of community building?

Anndrea: It does. I think it does. I was raised Baptist and then went to Catholic school in high school. It has actually helped a lot because there is a strong following of Catholicism in the community. It's been helpful to be able to know the power of the priests in the community. Where people are going for worship. Even having church services that took place at the Y for a certain time. To understand what that means, and that connection and piece is still able to exist, again, not excluding someone who doesn't necessarily fall into that group, is a very delicate but necessary and important piece of what we have to do at this YMCA and in this community.

Stephen: In your spiritual journey, you had said you were raised Baptist, but have you continued in that tradition? Have you grown and added belief systems to your spiritual path?

Anndrea: I don't know that I would say that I am going down that Baptist path. I would say I am more spiritual than religious. I am more faith-based than traditional or what religion brings to the table. I do believe that there is a higher power. Whether or not that is harnessed within each individual person or if there is a whole separate being that creates that. I guess that is a part of the learning and what it is I am seeking if you will. To have understanding.

Stephen: I have a question that is very relevant to this book. Do you believe in a soul, and if so, how would you describe it?

Anndrea: Yes. The easiest way I would describe it is a person's moral compass that guides them through life. After their physical being is exhausted and done, it's what continues on. Hopefully, the moral compass of whichever person, myself in this case, is guided in the appropriate direction. In a way, that leaves things better than they were found and understands compassion, people, and a greater appreciation for the things around them. Every day I say the serenity prayer. Some days I say "God." Some days I don't. In the end, I ask for different things, but it's the foundation that's the basis for what it is. We get so lost in the things we can't change and sometimes don't have the wherewithal to understand what those are—the things you can and can't change. The piece about having the courage to change the things you can is very important. Sometimes you can see what an issue is, but a lot of times people don't have the courage to say "let's go another way." I think that's what your soul is. While there is a physicality still associated with it, it's that thing that says we should go a different way.

Stephen: You said moral compass. Are we born with a moral compass? Are we given a moral compass by the people and environment around us?

Anndrea: I think both nature and nurture play a huge role. I think by nature, most living things have souls. I think that given the various experiences people go through in life, it can tilt that scale. Just like any other compass, it may need to be recalibrated. Depending on your experiences, you may come across an individual whose moral compass may need to be recalibrated.

Stephen: In the community you serve, there is crime, child poverty, alcohol, and drug abuse. All these issues we are always fighting against, and the Y is playing a role in some of those.

Anndrea: The Y should play a role . . . Just like any other community-based service organization. I think this is where the courage piece comes in, and sometimes some places don't want to touch certain things.

Stephen: You mean organizations need to have courage?

Anndrea: Yes, correct. Not just individually.

Stephen: I was going to ask, we were talking about this moral compass. There are people who are smoking crack and robbing people, shooting people. We know we are in the homicide capital of the country. It happens in Little Village and Pilsen as well. If we are talking about a moral compass, obviously those people have lost their compass. What do you think?

Anndrea: Well, this is obviously my personal opinion, but I think that sometimes some people have not been given the proper instructions on how to read their moral compass.

Stephen: So they have had it within them?

Anndrea: Just like a standard compass, if you don't understand north, south, east or west but let alone not know the direction you are supposed to be going in.

Stephen: You're not really going anywhere.

Anndrea: It doesn't make any difference. You are going to continue to spin around, and unfortunately, in the case of crime and the things that happen in this city, it seems as though a vicious cycle. There is nothing that breaks it . . . that shows it a different way or gives it a benefit of an alternative. Just like anything else, a lot of people want to know what the ROI is. If I don't know what the ROI is with me going down a different direction, I might as well go down this direction when I know what I'm gonna get. Whether it's beneficial for me or not. Whether it's detrimental for me or not. At least I know. Some people are more comfortable knowing their detriment than not knowing their triumph.

Stephen: Do you feel that these organizations are not doing enough, whether it's the YMCA or another organization?

Anndrea: I do think there is always opportunity to do more.

Stephen: That's a good segue to the next question. What are some of your greatest barriers or challenges that you have in this mission of serving people in your community?

Anndrea: I think, for one, establish trust within the community. It's a big thing for me personally as well for the organization I am with. There are organizations that have been around forever. Very deeply rooted and connected, Alevio . . . the Resurrection Project . . . Raul Raymundo, who is someone I recently met and has agreed to help mentor me and somebody I am learning to have a great deal of respect for as an individual and for who he is and who he represents in the community. To not have that history and connection is a big deal. Time is a big barrier . . . Resources. How to access resources. Not that so much the resources are unavailable. It's just a matter of how we access them.

Stephen: What are some of the issues you see that hold that from happening, finding a funding stream, finding resources?

Anndrea: Relationships . . . relationships, how to figure out how to get into that circle that will connect you to those resources. Because you can build a bridge, but if you don't have a start and an end point, how beneficial is your bridge? You could be a phenomenal architect, but if you don't have people that need to go from one place to the next . . .

Stephen: Do you think a lot of people come to communities such as Pilsen/Little Village and say, "We're going to build a bridge right here" or "This is what you need. You need a bridge from X to Y"?

Anndrea: I think that creates more barriers than it does opportunity. It perpetuates the distrust that communities such as Pilsen/Little Village have with outside influences. Instead of you coming in and finding out how you can be a part of the community, you come and assume you already know what this community needs. I don't think it's fair or responsible. I've seen it more so in Pilsen than Little Village. The word that people love to stay away from is called "gentrification." Sometimes I think that gentrification gets a bad rap. I do believe there are ways it can be beneficial to a community. It's the way it is approached and how people go about it.

Stephen: What is the gentrification issue in Pilsen to help us understand?

Anndrea: There are various developments taking place. When you talk to certain people in the community who don't feel that they were considered, and they will be able to afford to live there, and their children won't be able to afford to live there in the future.

You have student housing, which could be a good thing, but who are the students? There is one place that houses different students and was developed in a place people respect. This is how I know it can happen in a place and a space where people feel like they are a part of something and that they are helping or someone is coming back and reinvesting in their community. But nobody wants to feel abused. You know?

Stephen: University of Illinois at Chicago butts up against Pilsen, right?

Anndrea: It does, and that's a part of it. Your typical middle-class family may be different from what is considered middle class in this community. So that new student may have access and privilege that someone who grew up here doesn't.

Stephen: How do you think about all these issues and move the needle? To alleviate poverty, stop people from pulling the trigger, combat disparity. I know it is a complex question, but how do you create larger community impact? What's the secret sauce? What can we do differently?

Anndrea: Not to make sweeping judgements, but a true collaborative effort from the various organizations within the community. For people to leave their egos aside. To invite new people to the table. To respect and appreciate the seasoned people who have been at the table. So we don't overlap in resources. So we are not trying to do the same things. Also making sure that the people involved have knowledge and access. From there, you can assess, implement, and then reassess. You can't half step it. One thing I say to my siblings is you can't go from one to five without accounting for two, three, and four. You just can't do it. You may think you can do it, but at some point, you'll be going back to do two, three, and four.

Stephen: Time, in relation to what you are sharing, is very critical, but in our industry, there is a lot of turnover. The YMCA has a lot of turnover. These other nonprofits in Pilsen have a lot of turnover. It's like you have to back up and lose time. Or you lose the time you gained and have to start back at ground zero. This is a tough one for me. How do we solve that?

Anndrea: It goes back to that Maya Angelou quote, where it's something like "People don't care how much you know, they don't care what you say, what they care about is how you make them feel." I think that organizations have to start taking an inward look on how it is they are projecting outward and talk about what's really happening. The thing that I find to be most interesting about nonprofits or even for-profit companies, let's just say customer service organizations, is they are constantly looking at how you can do better for your customer, but the people who are actually doing the work are most often overlooked. If that person who is supposed to be making someone else feel good doesn't feel good, that transfer of energy is never going to happen. You got a problem. That synapse is not firing. You have got a serious disconnect. That's where we have to find out what is going on around you and with your team. Figure out how it is you're going to help them so, one, they can help themselves, and two, they can help someone else. Some of the most profound advice you get is when you take a flight. They tell you, "In the unlikely event the cabin pressure changes," and that little mask drops down, you need to secure your mask first before assisting others. Secure your mask first. That to me is so profound. That's life! [*Laughing*]

Stephen: Got to check yourself.

Anndrea: Before you wreck yourself. [*Laughing*]. You got to secure your own mask.

CHAPTER 12

An Inclusion Policy to Support Systems Change

I look forward confidently to the day when all who work for a living will be one with no thought to their separateness as Negroes, Jews, Italians or any other distinctions. This will be the day when we bring into full realization the American dream—a dream yet unfulfilled. A dream of equality of opportunity, of privilege and property widely distributed; a dream of a land where men will not take necessities from the many to give luxuries to the few; a dream of a land where men will not argue that the color of a man's skin determines the content of his character; a dream of a nation where all our gifts and resources are held not for ourselves alone, but as instruments of service for the rest of humanity; the dream of a country where every man will respect the dignity and worth of the human personality.
—Martin Luther King Jr.

My work in diversity and inclusion leadership over the years has had a profound effect on my life and my understanding of how we struggle to communicate, work, and interact personally and professionally but, more profoundly, how we design and implement strategies for poverty alleviation, economic development initiatives, youth violence prevention, and other initiatives within communities of need. The concept of using inclusive practices for developing a policy agenda or belief in engaging, valuing, respecting, and involving those who are being served in an atmosphere of trust and mutual respect is unfortunately a foreign concept to many working with struggling communities. There are those who have learned or understood from the beginning that working with communities of need requires solutions and activism to come from within the community. This does not exclude outside resources and support networks playing key roles, but lasting and systemic change must involve authentic ownership by the people being served. If there appears to be no local "harbormaster" or gem in the community, then those outside the community have not looked close enough. Informal leadership, role models, elders, and mentors always exist. It is paternalistic and arrogant to think that only an outside entity can provide solutions to long-term neighborhood and community problems. The answers are almost always able to be found organically and in small examples and programming on the local level, whether in churches, community centers, public parks, or the back room of a neighbor's home. Developing, expanding, and supporting these organic initiatives is the key to finding authentic and lasting solutions to community challenges.

This philosophy of community engagement can be seen in some locations but is rare as much of the funding, resources, and organizational leadership come from outside these communities of need. Organizations such as the Center for Neighborhood Enterprise and leaders such as Bob Woodson have built a strategy around mining, elevating, and supporting the "gems" that exist and are so often overlooked. In a recent trip to Kansas with the CNE team, we came across a local leader that was completely off the radar of the State Department of Family Services. My colleague and I questioned why, after speaking with him in the parking lot of the church where our summit was taking place, he had not been invited to this critical gathering of community leaders, church groups, and organizations. Phil, we found out that day, was a local resident who had recently purchased an abandoned property and was turning it into a metal shop and mechanic training facility. As a mechanic himself, Phil realized that he had the ability to train and teach a valuable skill to local residents and provide them with an opportunity for economic mobility. How do the Phils of the world get plugged into the resources, support networks, and assistance if they are not visible or actively sought out?

This is why we need to take a philosophical step back as the "provider establishment" and service sector and practice an inclusive strategy of poverty alleviation and community development. We have to find new and innovative ways to channel funding from our traditional sources directly to those "harbormasters" in the community while providing support, technical assistance, and resources to ensure successful programmatic outcomes and implementation.

There are five basic principles that must be followed if we are going to be able to begin to make a shift in how we think, function, and fund initiatives and create true inclusive and grassroots policy strategies.

We must learn to listen, value, appreciate, and engage one another in honest and sincere ways that promote candid dialogue, conversation, and understanding.

I find it interesting that this concept of authentic listening and communication is one of the most critical aspects of success in the workplace. Something that would seem so simple and easy. Something that should come naturally to us and without difficulty. Wasn't it taught to us in preschool, kindergarten, and grade school? Playing in the sandbox together and not throwing metaphorical sand in one another's eyes. You would think that these early lessons would have sunken in and become second nature to us. Unfortunately, this is not the case. In my experience, whether in the corporate world at a Fortune 500 company or an inner-city not-for-profit organization, it is the single most challenging aspect of creating successful systems, processes, and programmatic operations. Why has this become so hard for us as adults? Why have we become so rigid, stubborn, and opinionated in our thinking?

Many of us have to relearn how to learn. Rethink how we operate and interact with one another. The need for many in the workplace to hold on to known ways of operating and holding to the status quo, combined with the resistance to innovation and change, perpetuates silos, creates poor organizational culture and breeds ineffective communication. We have become so cemented in our own philosophy and way of being that we oftentimes limit ourselves from new learning, rarely allowing ourselves to be wrong and struggle with deeper levels of partnership and collaboration. In fact, organizational structures and systems have been built to support this attitude and way of noninclusive behavior.

We must be patient with the effort of cultural and spiritual transformation and not become disillusioned. It took centuries to create our situation. It will take more than one or two generations to repair.

Many times, we can become easily frustrated and impatient when we are a part of a dysfunctional or broken system. We actually have the right to be frustrated, and many of us who have been disenfranchised, locked out, or discriminated against, even persecuted in that system, have a right to be angry and voice opinions and opposition as guaranteed in the First Amendment of the constitution. Protest, activism, and the mobilization of people is necessary and a strong part of our American identity. At times, progress is slow and tedious and takes the work and voice of many. We all have to become committed to being a part of the process of change and doing our part, recognizing that change takes time; and our perseverance, consistency, and passion is what will ultimately bring us to a different place. It is the same within communities or organizations. Effort, consistency, and persistence is important. Change and progress marches step by step, often slowly and with great resistance; but as water can drip from a gutter on a stone floor and cause an indentation over time, so can our perseverance and long-term effort create the change we desire in ourselves, our larger communities, and our world.

Faith and hope play a strong role in this process, regardless of religious or spiritual affiliation. The belief in change is the precursor to that change manifesting. Our ability to engage in intentional actions, founded in the belief in those actions, is at the very root of our ability as human beings to grow, transform, and elevate our reality.

We must work harder to listen to our shared spiritual yearning for values most everyone regard: love, peace, friendship, caring, and authentic human connection.

Beyond all the dogma and hard-line opinions and beliefs is something deeper that binds us together as human beings. Some may not have the willingness or ability to recognize it, yet it is there. A deeper consciousness and yearning for connectivity, a yearning for purpose, and a higher existence void of hate, hunger, poverty, and violence. It is what I call a soulful purpose, a deeper connection to our shared spiritual selves.

Many in our society seem to have lost the concept of empathy, to understand, to know your brother and sister as yourself. What could possibly allow one human being to look someone in the eye and pull a trigger and take another life? The violence we see today, especially in our inner cities, seems more pervasive and raw, perpetrated by younger, more hopeless people than we have seen in the past. Reaching those most lost or most disenfranchised will undoubtedly take persistence, commitment, and an acknowledgement that all cannot be saved. Faith in our ability to overcome struggle and a journey toward a deeper soul-filled connection, and spiritual understanding must be part of the solution.

As a grove of aspen trees can be connected through their root system and form one larger singular organism invisible aboveground, I believe we, as human beings, have been given an innate ability to connect spiritually to one another through a deeper consciousness rooted in the concepts of love, friendship, caring, and peace. It is there in the soul of all of us—it has simply yet to be awoken in many of us.

We must recognize our shared history as an American people and the systems of oppression that have been created by that history.

We must once and for all accept and own our shared history in this country. Acknowledge the crimes and atrocities against our indigenous populations, the evil and horrific legacy of slavery of black Americans, and the marginalization of women and the LGBTQ community, just to name a few. Unfortunately, the list is quite long, but not only to acknowledge the horrors and transgressions of the past but also how those actions, policies, and practices created, over hundreds of years, a system of institutionalized inequity and injustice that has had lasting implications on the issues and challenges of our current day.

White folks, we must bear this burden of our American past in order to move forward into a different future. A future of equity and equality. A future of atonement and rebirth. White people must acknowledge their fear of moving from a dominant culture to one that is fast become a minority within our population such as in the state of California. This shift of power and status has caused fear and frustration. We must own this and move forward together. Moving forward together in a way where we can walk side by side on an equal footing with communities of color, with the sun shining in *all* our faces and a wind behind *all* of our backs.

Those of power and privilege can be a part of the efforts of change. We can help fuel the tank but must relinquish our control of the wheel and be willing to take the back seat and at times not get in the car at all.

These principles are much easier to understand and apply in theory but incredibly difficult to bring into practice and continue over time. It is the very nature of our hierarchical and oppressive systems that inhibit the application of these principles. We can look at examples of the American justice system, health care system, public educational system, financial system, and, of course, our political system. They were all built on foundations of oppression and economic and racial inequity. Structures that have been embedded with historical context and experience of inequality and injustice.

The relinquishing and sharing of power, acknowledgment of privilege, and actual change and shift in functional behavior is extremely difficult for individuals but even more difficult for organizations, corporations, and governmental structures. It is however, only through the conscious choice of those in power and privilege to give up power and give authentic voice, access, and opportunity to those traditionally left out or disenfranchised that we can begin to walk down a different path, a path toward true equity and equality.

This book is hopefully seen as a call to action and a call to all of us for a deep reflective breath. To take a look at not only our individual actions and role we can each play in making change in the world around us, but how we can change the systems and structures we have built as a culture and society. Though our individual spiritual and emotional growth is critical to this change, it has to move beyond the individual journey to a more empathetic, intentional, and transformational space. In a 1967 speech at Riverside Church, Dr. Martin Luther King Jr. said the following:

> A true revolution of values will cause us to question the fairness and justice of many of our past and present policies. On the one hand we are called to play the good Samaritan on life's roadside, but that will only be an initial act. One day we must come to see that the whole Jericho Road must be transformed so that men and women will not be constantly beaten and robbed as they make their journey on life's highway. True compassion is more than flinging a coin to a beggar. It comes to see that an edifice which produces beggars needs restructuring.

Martin Luther King Jr. was obviously a person who was transformational in our modern culture and able to see far beyond the issues of his own time. His words are as relevant today as they were during the civil rights movement of the late '60s. However, it is time to move beyond words and do the difficult work of changing our hearts and begin connecting to one another in ways that we have not yet achieved. Only this deeper connection can create the collective power to change the structures and systems within which we operate. If we do not change directions and walk toward this path, a much more violent social unrest and upheaval is unfortunately sure to come.

CHAPTER 13

Antwan Diggs

Buffalo, New York

He said, "Because you have so little faith. I tell you the truth, if you have
faith as small as a mustard seed, you can say to this mountain, 'Move from
here to there' and it will move. Nothing will be impossible for you."
—Matthew 17:20

I met Antwan Diggs in 2003 during a youth summit sponsored by the
Department of Justice. I was hired as a consultant with the Center for
Neighborhood Enterprise working with a program called Weed and Seed,
where we were working with teens from around the country and developing
their leadership skills and providing mentorship opportunities. Antwan
brought fifteen youth with him in a passenger van from Buffalo, New York
to Phoenix, Arizona, for our seven-day youth summit. I learned later that
he had a fear of flying and would not take a flight. Over the years, I have
worked with Antwan as a facilitator and consultant on various training
and youth development initiatives. He is a passionate advocate, pastor, and
mentor for youth on their journey toward adulthood. It was very clear from
the first meeting that he was dedicated to his work and was the type of
leader with a great story to tell. I would not learn about the full extent of
this fascinating story until my interview for this book in 2015. He currently
works for the City of Buffalo, New York, and is married with two beautiful
children. Above all, I have known Antwan to be a man of God and a strong
believer in his Christian faith. This interview took place in Salina, Kansas,
at a Holiday Inn restaurant that served some especially tasty hamburgers.

Stephen: Tell me about who you are, some of your background, and what you do in the community.

Antwan: So I am from Philadelphia, Pennsylvania, in a place known as the Black Bottom. It's officially called Manchua, but people who know in Philly, West Philadelphia, call it the Bottom. Those of us from the Bottom know of it as the Black Bottom. It's predominantly an African American community. Growing up there, I never thought of class. The only reference I had to living a little better than somebody else was a candy store we used to go to called Cuz's. He would treat those of us who weren't from the projects different from those who were in the projects. He seemed to think that project kids acted differently. He was a black man who owned the store. We lived around the corner, and he seemed to think the project kids didn't respect him. We had family who lived in the projects, but not our family, but you couldn't tell us that we didn't know 'cause if you could go up there and make it to the seventeenth floor, you were pretty much in. People didn't just go in there. You had to know somebody.

I lived in a house with my mother and father. She was a seamstress, and he was in the army. When he came back from the army, he worked for Conrail. I watched my dad get up every morning and put on a starched white shirt and jacket. When I was privileged to go to work with him, he was in charge. All these white people riding the train, and he was in charge. All these people, old, young, rich, my dad had some power. He was the conductor, and they had to pay him . . . Get a ticket or he would put them off the train. Years passed, and I started to grow up. I was always active in the community. One of my first jobs as an entrepreneur was selling soda at the park. I would go to the store and sell them for a ten-cent profit at the park.

Stephen: How old were you?

Antwan: I must have been seven or eight.

Stephen: A businessman at seven, huh?

Antwan: I did that till I was about ten, and then I went to the local grocery store bagging groceries. We lived around the corner, so I knew everyone in the neighborhood. I had the opportunity to meet some young brothers that were doing some great stuff in the community. I got on this committee when I was about fourteen or fifteen. They were doing something about graffiti. The next year, the first black mayor of the City of Philadelphia took the head of that committee and made him a commissioner. As he moved up, we moved up. I was volunteering as a youth member in city hall doing good stuff in the neighborhood. I got my first official letter from city hall. It had a gold stamp from the mayor saying I was appointed as a youth commissioner. You couldn't tell me anything. I was so proud my head just would swell up.

Stephen: So that's not a typical thing a kid does at that age . . . being socially active and involved in committees doing positive things for your neighborhood. Is this something you got from your parents?

Antwan: It came from the neighborhood. I grew up where they had gang warfare. There were serious turf issues. We had places called Up the Way, Down the Way, the Empire. There were blocks you could not go. This stuff didn't register with me. I would go wherever I wanted. It may have come from living behind the playground and watching people. I was bored, and my parents would think I was at the playground around the corner, but I was twenty or thirty blocks away. I was a people person. I would just walk around and meet people.

Stephen: But the social consciousness just came from yourself?

Antwan: I guess so. It was just always in me. These young brothers I connected with were in their early twenties. They definitely played a role.

Stephen: So they were doing a lot of positive stuff?

Antwan: Yes, all positive stuff. When I got hooked up with these guys, instead of going into the gym in the community center, I would go upstairs and hang out on the phones with these guys answering community calls. I would take messages and answer phone calls. They weren't paying me. I was just volunteering, but they noticed something in me. They realized I would come and conduct myself appropriately. When I had to work, I would work, but I wanted to be a part of what they were doing. When the head guy, Tim Spencer, got moved to the mayor's office, everyone went with him, I guess trying to get jobs. I was too young. I still went with them and volunteered at the city hall. I didn't share much with my family. They thought I was going to school, but I would sneak out and go to the city hall in a shirt and tie. I didn't want to go to school.

Stephen: So what about your parents?

Antwan: The experience of living in the Black Bottom, we owned our own house, but there were times when lights were off. We weren't rich. We weren't middle class. We were maybe a step above the projects, but my experience was I would come home, my mom and dad would drink, and sometimes they fought. So I stayed away from the house. I had a fear that I would see them fight and really go at it and see lights flashing one day.

Stephen: Would you say they were alcoholics?

Antwan: Well, you know, I can't call them alcoholics. My mom still drinks. Let me fast forward a bit. Somewhere around eighteen or nineteen years old, the people whom I had been working with, Tim Spencer and others, ran into my dad at the bar. He was telling my dad all about the great things I was doing in the community. My dad said, "Well, that's interesting, because I just received a call from the school that my son is flunking out of high school because he's not showing up." He blew Tim away because he thought I was taking care of my business. He thought I was a good student.

One day he called me in and said, "You can't serve with us anymore until you bring us a report card and I know you are doing okay in school." It was a rap. I was done with that volunteer work at the city hall. I was upset and thought, *Well, if I can't hang out with these guys, I'll find some other people to hang with.* These were people who drank beer, smoked weed, and snorted coke. I eventually started smoking crack. It was called freebasing back then in the '80s.

Stephen: This was when you were seventeen?

Antwan: By nineteen, I was a full-fledged crackhead. By eighteen, everyone knew I was strung out. All the people I knew before as someone who was doing something positive now knew me as a basehead.

Stephen: That's a complete about-face. You were an activist, positive and focused. How did you change so quickly?

Antwan: I guess when he shut me down . . . He was my role model. He shattered me because he called me out. I was crushed.

Stephen: So this guy you looked up to shut you out, but you said you looked up to your dad, too. Why did you fall so far . . . What about your parents?

Antwan: You have to understand these were the years where crack was running rampant in the community. At the beginning of those years, the early '80s, my daily network became all these people hiding around doing drugs. I was working and doing catering and made some money, but we were at the sets, buying eight balls. We thought we were cool. The next thing I know, I'm only thinking about what I can do to get to the next party. It then started to become not about the next party but just about the next high. Now my whole set changed. I went from going to people's houses partying to going into holes and sneaking around looking for crack cocaine.

Stephen: So I have to ask this question . . . I have known you now for years as a man of God, a man who mentors children, who is changing people's lives for the better. How long were you in this place? How did you get out?

Antwan: It got so bad I don't remember the year, but I remember the day. It got progressively worse. After about three or four years, it got so bad I couldn't come home. Once I did get home and my uncle found my stash . . . my bags, scales, and vials of crack in a briefcase in my bedroom. I was about twenty-one or twenty-two. Once that happened, that was it. My mom couldn't deny what was happening. I knew right then and there I was going to try to get myself together. I had a chance to go to New York with some people, so I went. I wanted to escape but also prove to my mom I could make it in New York and call her and say, "Mom, come visit. I made it."

Stephen: So you wanted to get sober?

Antwan: Yeah, but little did I know that I was going from the frying pan and into the fire.

With crack in Philly, I was paying five to ten dollars a bag. In Harlem, they had bags twice the size for two and three dollars. I started hanging with guys that were doing more and more often than I ever did. I started panhandling, begging for money. My number for the day was eight dollars. This is how bad it got. Once I got eight dollars, I could go to the crack house, buy four bags, give one to the house, and sit for a few hours and get high. I would go back downtown in the afternoon and do the same thing again. This lasted for six to seven years until I literally got locked up in jail.

Stephen: How long were you locked up for?

Antwan: I got three and a half years for assault and strong-armed robbery and went from Rikers' Island to upstate New York. I had a couple other arrests, so this one stuck.

Stephen: How old were you when you went to Rikers?

Antwan: I was about twenty-three or twenty-four. My first day, I saw a fight between two guys. The correction officers were letting them go at it. I just went into my cell and started to pray.

Stephen: So this is the first time I heard you say anything about prayer. How did your connection with God begin?

Antwan: My dad was a Baptist, I was baptized in the church he attended. This was when I was in my early days. I wanted to join the choir, but for some reason, they didn't want to have me involved. I tried to join the choir in a Lutheran church, but for some reason, they said no. I was pretty turned off and never went back. I remember being in the bathroom one day praying to God to not have my dad whip me. I guess I had gotten into trouble at school. My dad would regularly get the belt and give a lecture, and then a week or two of punishment. For whatever reason, that day, he just walked out of the house and didn't touch me. I knew God answered me that day.

Stephen: So I want to fast-forward to your first day in prison when you said you prayed to God for help. You had been doing crack for the last seven years, robbing people, stealing. Why did you think God would suddenly answer you or come to your side?

Antwan: I guess I had a God conscience. That I could have a connection and conversation with God even though I was lost. The Bible talks about having mustard-seed-sized faith. I was so aware of God's' presence. I remember I would walk by churches, not go in, but touch the edges of the walls. I would literally walk around the face of the church to touch each side. At the last edge, I would say, "Lord please help me." I knew nothing about the church. There was just a God connection. Someone was watching over me and knew who I was and what I was doing. If I was hungry, I would find a sandwich. If I was cold, I would find a jacket. An answer to a prayer.

Stephen: So how did you survive in jail for three and a half years?

Antwan: Once I got sentenced at Rikers, I went to upstate New York to finish my time. The recommendation was eight and a half to twenty-five years. The only reason he was lenient, he said, was because of my demeanor in court that day. I sat reading my Bible, was calm and collected. So I went upstate. It was there I started searching and looking for answers. I sat with the Muslims, sat with the Christian scientists, the Catholic church, but nothing seemed right. One day, there was a Protestant service. There was a volunteer who came from the outside. I asked, "How do you expect us to get all this?"

He said, "Calm down, brother, don't try to digest it all at once. Why don't you just start with the gospels and look at the character of Jesus . . . Matthew, Mark, Luke, and John."

I asked, "Are you going to be here next week?"

He said, "God willing." This was the first time I began really studying the Bible and the Word.

Stephen: So when did you feel you wanted to serve others and start giving back?

Antwan: I got assigned at the program committee and was told I needed a high school diploma if I wanted a better position. The woman told me I needed to go to GED classes if I wanted a better job and higher salary. She said, "Go get your GED, and I will bring you back and get you a better position." So I got my GED in a few months and got a position helping with orientation. I had to show videos to new people coming into prison. I asked if I could change up the presentation where we didn't just show a boring video but actually talked to the new inmates. The supervisor came and watched me. I would introduce him. He would say a few words, and that's how it went. It was my first training job. [*Laughing*] I was empowered. Before I knew it, I was looking to go back to school. I got college credit for taking classes in prison.

Stephen: So prison actually worked for you?

Antwan: I wasn't arrested. I was rescued. I get to Watertown (upstate), and I was getting up in the morning. I had a job. I was going to school. I got my GED. I was studying the Bible. Life was changing. I spoke to the superintendent, I told him I had plans. I asked, "If I get parole, will you write me a letter of recommendation for the outside?"

He said, "I can't write one prior to parole, but if you get paroled, I will write you a letter." So I was released three and a half years after I was arrested and ended up in a shelter in New York.

Stephen: So you are a minister now. You are a youth mentor now. How has all this helped you in the work you do now in the community?

Antwan: It is the foundation for everything that I do. When I look back, I say that it is the experience that allows me to understand. To learn from my mistakes. The Bible says that God takes all things and works them out. There is nothing that is past, present, and future that he will not work out. My pastor told me one day that I was one of God's treasures. It took me a while to understand that. I finally understood that when you look at trophy cases, you don't see the hard work that went into achieving that trophy. You don't see the ups and downs and struggles it took. The story that goes behind the trophy. I am a mentor, a father, a husband, a community leader. I am a better individual. Everything that I went through has been my class for service and serving others. I can serve from the "greatest of these to the least of these" because he has blessed me.

Stephen: How did you get to Buffalo from New York City?

Antwan: I had relapsed in New York and finally got an opportunity to go to a place called Hope House run by Sister Karen Klimczak. She ran the "Home of Positive Experiences." This place was like a mansion. I got a key, my own room. She did something to my heart. She eventually gave me a key to the pantry. I couldn't believe it. She was basically like "mi casa su casa." She eventually opened up the teen center. Brand-new stuff. New computers, gaming stations, it was beautiful.

Stephen: What was the name of the teen center?

Antwan: St. Columba Bridgid Teen Center, the same center I work at now. She said, "Here is the key and the alarm code. I want you to run the center on Friday and Saturday nights."

I thought to myself, *If I relapse, I am going to sell all this stuff.* But the more she trusted me, the more I didn't want to disappoint her. This white nun, this sister . . . I wasn't Catholic, but she supported me going to the Baptist church down the street. She knew the pastor.

Stephen: So this is the same place you have been for seventeen years. Your entire career developed off this experience?

Antwan: My whole career started right there. She was murdered in 2006. Somebody sent the news to me, and I went over there and was interviewed. I told them my story. Someone put it in the local paper. The same story I am telling you. I had been working in the city hall for three or four years by then. I realized that God had given me a gift to share my story. Not to brag or boast, I don't share it with everybody.

Stephen: So at the teen center, when was the first time you felt like you helped another person or kid and played a part in changing their lives?

Antwan: So I was working for a program called the Youth Opportunity Program. The federal government had given Buffalo like $25 million over a five-year period to work with youth all over the city. We worked with youth, found them jobs, helped them to find direction. The kids that were coming to the program had an opportunity to work all year long. They were connected to me in after school programming, and they would work. In the summer, we would take them on leadership summits around the country. This was paid for by Weed and Seed dollars. It was a national program that worked with local law enforcement to weed out crime and then seed in programs and initiatives to provide hope and opportunities. There was this one kid, Christian, I think you met him. He was a computer genius. When it came to computers, he just got it. So I took him around with grant money I had, and he repaired computers, and we paid him. He just took to it. He would pick up my bag, shake my hand. He gave me a firm handshake every time I saw him. There was something about him. Since he started working, he hasn't stopped.

Stephen: How old is he now?

Antwan: He has to be twenty-five or twenty-six. Now these kids are giving it back to others. All the things we did, they are now giving back to others in the community. I haven't really thought about it, but it's powerful.

It's' crazy even how I got to Buffalo at all. Back in prison, I was talking to some Christian brothers about leaving jail in ninety days, and I just knew that I didn't want to go back to New York. I met this one guy who overheard the brothers talking about my situation. He apparently was heading to Hope House in Buffalo but got another twenty-four months somehow and lost his spot. He said, "Why don't you give Buffalo a try if you have nowhere to go?" He gave me the opportunity by giving me his letter.

I called Sister Karen in Buffalo. She said, "I can't give you a bed. You have to go through the process with parole." That's what I set out to do, but the law says you have to go back to the county where you were arrested. That was New York City. I prayed. I listened to Bible tapes. I was told I would have to write a letter and get special approval to leave the county of commitment. I wrote the letter but later found out it was never mailed. A few weeks later, I was called to the administration building. I thought to myself, *Why am I going to the administration building?*

When I walked across the yard, I noticed the sun . . . warm on my skin, huge . . . like I could just reach out and touch it. I thought, "Wow, God is awesome." It was beautiful. It was one of those timeless moments. I got to the building, and there was a lady there. I had no idea who she was. She asked, "Are you Antwan Diggs?"

I said, "Yes."

She said, "I've been on the phone all day long, begging and pleading with somebody to let you go to Buffalo. You better go to Buffalo, and you better not mess up!" She turned around and slammed the door. I never saw her again.

Stephen: The rest is history?

Antwan: The rest is history.

CHAPTER 14

Transformational Leadership

To lead people, walk behind them.

—Lao Tzu

The concept of transformational leadership, or lack of, is clearly front and center in the 2016 political campaign season. Donald Trump and the GOP have made a mockery of the prestige and seriousness of the American political process and presidency. So much so that the GOP establishment is walking away from their own party. Our Democratic leadership also leaves much to be desired. How we select our political leadership and what their qualifications may or may not be has been hotly and, at times, vigorously debated. This year, however, our nation has reached a new low in political discourse. Ten-second media sound bites, 140-character Twitter feeds, and divisive and mean-spirited rants verging on hate-speech hardly equate to political discourse.

In understanding and elevating the concept of transformational leadership, the word needs to be defined separately and then revisited as a larger concept:

Transform: To make a thorough or dramatic change in the form, appearance, or character of.

Lead: To show the way to by going in advance: the host led us to our table. To guide or direct in a course of action.

In my many years of work in large systems, nonprofit organizational management, and community development, the concept of transformational leadership has recently been elevated in my mind. In preparing for and teaching a course at the University of Chicago at the School of Social Service Administration titled "Nonprofit Management: Creating Systemic Change and Community Empowerment," I realized that a section of my syllabus must be on transformational leadership and how to apply and challenge oneself as a leader to embody the principles that the words represent. Organizational and community leadership must work to change systems and encourage people to create a more positive atmosphere for growth, development, and the inspiration of others. If we do not embrace this approach, as leaders, we are not truly leading the organization and those who are there for us to lead on a path of transformation and change. In many companies, organizations, and civic institutions, we see a mind-set of complacency and support of the status quo. Most people are comfortable with what is and what has been, the accepted practices that govern the work we do, even if we know we are not achieving the highest level of success possible. People generally fear what is unknown and different. We are comfortable in the structures and patterns we have created for ourselves because it is familiar and comforting. Whenever someone new enters an existing system, a different set of eyes can view that system or situation with a different lens and perspective.

Transformational Leadership is defined as a leadership approach that causes change in individuals and social systems. In its ideal form, it creates valuable and positive change in the followers with the end goal of developing followers into leaders.

In my years as an executive leader, I have been brought into various organizations with the task of creating change, elevating productivity, enhancing financial capacity, and encouraging a culture of inclusion and opportunity. This is easier said than done. Many times, issues of privilege and power, race, seniority, personal agenda, and the desire to perpetuate the status quo will challenge the ability of a new leader to effectively make changes and promote growth. Ultimately, as in most relational issues, the development of trust is the critical factor to success.

There is a learning model that was shared in the book *Presence: An Exploration of Profound Change in People, Organizations and Society*, written by Peter Senge, that was critical in explaining the challenges of organizational change and understanding people's desire to hold on to the status quo or that which is comfortable, easy, and understood. Senge shares the concept that when we challenge ourselves to grow and learn and take on new approaches to functioning or solving problems, we enter unknown territory, which can elicit fear and defensiveness in many people. Most people tend to want to stay in a place of comfort and control. However, it is the very ability to help people see their own need to grow and develop, which can, in turn, help the organization to embrace change. This process can often be met with resistance and be seen as threatening to the organization's operational status quo. Transformational leadership and effective organizational change is built on trust, and this can take time to develop. Trust is promoted by consistency, integrity, transparency, and fairness. It is also built over time through a transformational leader's' ability to demonstrate results and put into practice the principles they espouse.

> Deeper levels of learning create increasing awareness of the larger whole—both as it is and as it is evolving—that leads to actions that increasingly serve the emerging whole. (*Presence*, Peter Senge)

Thinking about how individuals or silos in an organization can work together more effectively is common in many industries, not just the nonprofit sector. There has been much research about this topic and books written on the topics of collaboration and change management. Thinking about how we learn and process organizational challenges and opportunities and serving the "whole organization" as opposed to parts is an effective way to begin the process of understanding the silo phenomenon. Many organizations do not take adequate time to discuss this concept and work through the barriers that exist within the organizational and interpersonal structures within which we operate. Transformational leaders utilize staff and leadership development, training, and individual supervision to elevate these organizational issues and consistently work toward the removal of the barriers that are in place and impeding organizational growth.

A short excerpt from the foreword from the book *Presence* is very insightful in this regard:

> Our normal way of thinking cheats us. It leads to think of wholes as made up of many parts, the way a car is made up of wheels, a chassis, and a drive train. In this way of thinking, the whole is assembled from the parts and depends upon them to work effectively. If a part is broken,

it must be repaired or replaced. This is a very logical way of thinking about machines. But living systems are different.

Unlike machines, living systems, such as your body or a tree, create themselves. They are not mere assemblages of their parts but are continually growing and changing along with their elements.

The process of "unlearning" the ways we have traditionally been taught to think and function in team environments is a challenge to many institutions. Many of us have fallen into a pattern of operation that is contrary to the ideals of collaboration and partnership. These "silos," as they have been commonly referred to, are actually supported by our current ways of thinking and are comfortable and safe as they do not challenge us to move beyond what we know and trust. Our resistance to fuller and richer collaboration is rooted deep in our thinking, our subconscious brain, that resists change, limits innovation, and fears failure. At a more basic and conscious level, we tend to lack familiarity, comfort, and trust in the workplace. This is even more true when we may be perceived as different or indeed be different from our colleagues in terms of gender, race, culture, class, and ways of thinking and operating.

Transformational leaders must recognize the need for innovative thinking and be willing to help others relearn old ways of operating and interacting. The ability to lead others through change processes, growth, and innovation is at the core of a transformational leader's' work. This demands inclusive practices that values the voice of other perspectives, engages others, and constantly demonstrates respect. Ultimately, a transformational leader understands the needs of those in the change process, addresses those needs through building trust, but continues to move the organizational vision forward and retaining the right to make difficult decisions.

There is a short story I used in a class I taught at the University of Chicago's School of Social Service Administration called "Now We Must Cross the Sea: Remarks on Transformational Leadership and the Civil Rights Movement," which is truly an inspiring story of leadership and the work and effort that is taken to not only transform mind-sets but also lead people through the journey of a long-term struggle and distant destination.

Now We Must Cross the Sea (Walter Earl Fluker, original story by Lerone Bennett)

Once upon a time long ago in a land far away, there lived a brave captain and a courageous crew of women and men who were in search of a new land. Standing on the shores of their land far away and a long time ago, this brave captain said to his courageous crew, the new land which we seek is far beyond the horizon, as our fathers and mothers spoke of it. It was the land which was promised to us, a land of freedom and harmony among peoples of the earth; and in order to reach this land we must cross an ocean and a sea. The journey, he said, will be long and difficult and many who start with us will not make it to the shore of the new land. The waters that we must sail are treacherous, storms rage there, the winds are mighty and chilling, fierce bandits and pirates also sail these hazardous waters, and I want you to know I might not reach this land with you. But if anything should happen to me along the way, you must continue the journey for surely the land awaits us as our forebears promised, a land of freedom and harmony among the peoples of the Earth. So it was from these shores in this land far away and in this time long ago that this brave captain and his courageous crew of women and men set sail for the new land, the land which was promised by their mothers and fathers. And true to the captain's words, the journey was long and difficult, the waters were treacherous, the storms raged, the winds were mighty and chilling; fierce bandits and pirates assailed their small vessel, and many lives were lost in the dark and cold abyss beneath them. But a small remnant did make it to the shores of the new land. The captain, though wounded in battle and broken from the long days and even longer nights of the voyage, did make it to the shores with his crew. The small remnant of courageous men and women who had endured the terrible onslaught of the ocean, and the devastating nightmare of battles on the water, shouted in celebration because they had finally made it to the land which they sought, the land which their forbears had promised. But as he lay dying, the captain, with bated breath hardly above a whisper, said to them, "This is not a time for celebration; it is not the time to rest, for the journey doesn't end here.

We have only crossed the ocean, now you must cross a sea."

The civil rights movement and subsequent strides and regressions in equality and justice in our nation are a good example of the long-term process and difficulty in creating sustainable and lasting change in organizations and large systems. While the specific legal strides and changes in law born from years of struggle and dissent like the Civil Rights Act are only part of the journey. An important part for sure, but the second step, the more difficult step, is known as the Non-Enforceable Demand. This is something that Martin Luther King Jr. called *excessive altruism.* "It is a purely spontaneous, unmotivated, groundless and creative act which arises out of genuine concern for the neighbor." This cannot be forced upon us by a law, act, or decree but must be motivated by "unenforceable, self-imposed, inner sanctions." I would call this "self-imposed, inner sanction," our soul consciousness, that leads us to a higher place of understanding, community, and interaction with those who walk among us on this earth.

The story of this captain from "Now We Must Cross the Sea" does a good job of demonstrating transformational leadership, one that holds to the highest levels of integrity and commitment. A leader showing favoritism to one over another, a leader who puts in less work or effort then their crew, or a leader who goes back on their word, or is not respected in their role cannot be a transformational leader. The idea is to pass on all that is best in you as both a human being and professional. To give all of yourself in the journey and to be accountable to those you have been charged to lead. As with Dr. King and the civil rights movement, a leader must see the longer struggle within the context of the individual hurdles and challenges of every day. This level of leadership takes wisdom, experience, and time to cultivate. Though these leaders, as all people, are fallible and make mistakes and are not immune from error, it is a transformational leader's job to recognize their error, acknowledge it, and learn from it. If necessary, apologize for it to those deserving of the apology. To always remain humble.

The individuals that have been interviewed and written about in this book are excellent examples of transformational leaders. They embody the values that elevate our consciousness and connection to our individual and deeper collective purpose. A soul-filled purpose that recognizes the need to empower those around them. In reality, much is gained in return by the transformational leader in this effort, as many of the stories in these chapters have expressed. Transformational leadership takes persistence, intention, dedication, and a willingness to learn through the process of change, walking through the challenges and successes. Ultimately, transformational leaders must be continually growing individually and in solidarity with those in their sphere of influence.

CHAPTER 15

Mariana Osoria

Chicago, Illinois

We cannot seek achievement for ourselves and forget about progress and prosperity for our community . . . Our ambitions must be broad enough to include the aspirations and needs of others, for their sakes and for our own.
—Cesar Chavez

Mariana Osoria and I have known each other since our early twenties. We began our respective careers in the world of casework with the Department of Children and Family Services in Chicago's Latino community, advocating for children and families within the juvenile justice system. Over the years, our careers have paralleled each other, even spending five years on the same team working for a school-based nonprofit called Youth Guidance, serving children and families within the Chicago public school system as counselors and therapists. We both graduated from the School of Social Service Administration at the University of Chicago. While we have moved in similar circles, worked on community development projects, fought for disenfranchised populations, and even become executive leaders in the same West Side community, we have always remained close friends. Our families have enjoyed time together, watching our children grow, sharing and connecting through good and bad times. The most powerful aspect of my knowing Mariana is her passion for serving her community, her commitment to her culture, and her tenacity and work ethic. She is a true champion of those in need and a leader who inspires and motivates others. We met recently for breakfast at the Golden Nugget restaurant in the Logan Square/Hermosa community in Chicago's Northwest Side to conduct this interview.

Stephen: Mariana . . . tell me about who you are, your background, and a bit about what you do.

Mariana: Well . . . I am Mariana Osoria. I am currently a vice president, one of two regional vice presidents of Family Focus, a nonprofit in Chicago. I'll tell you a little bit about how I got to where I am now. I studied fashion design in college, but when I finished my BA, I had to get a job that paid the bills . . . However, I think I always had a sense of giving back, wanting to be a part of the community, but I never had the language or the understanding around what that was. That you could actually have a career in that field. I come from an immigrant family. My father was an immigrant from Mexico. He had a pretty strict idea of what you could do for a career . . . a doctor, a lawyer, and an architect.

Stephen: A fashion designer was not one of those things?

Mariana: Definitely not. With that said . . . I did end up convincing him to let me study fashion design . . . I guess he thought that I was being, you know, part of an immigrant family, wanting to be entrepreneurial and successful. All along, my father was very active in the community. He was part of a nonprofit group. He was a volunteer. He always talked to us about what it meant to be an immigrant, a Mexican in the United States. He was the first person who introduced me to the word "Chicana." He always said, "You are a Chicana." He always had some sort of community involvement. I remember from very young, on the weekends, he would take us to a place where he volunteered, and trucks would come in with food, bread, basic items, and "the government cheese." All kinds of stuff. We would pack things in grocery bags. We would do it early in the morning, and people would come later in the day. I can just remember how thankful people were.

Stephen: How old were you when you first recall this experience?

Mariana: I'm not quite sure . . . I must have been around nine or ten. We always had a very close family. There was always this underlying civic responsibility, but never specific language about what we had to do about it, just kind of talking about where we come from, how we should be treated and treat others. The other thing I remember was when my father was very involved in the mayoral campaign during the Harold Washington election. I was probably eleven or twelve at that time. I was in this hotel when Jane Byrne, Richard Daley, and Harold Washington were having this debate. Of course, I didn't comprehend everything going on, but I distinctly remember the energy in the room when Harold Washington was speaking. How the room was, the sounds in the room, it was motivating, and I was greatly impacted by how one person could motivate people and get this type of energy going. This has always stuck with me. As I learned more about the process and the coalition building that he had, how he brought African Americans, Latinos, and Anglos together . . . it just stuck with me. Eventually, I spoke with some friends in the nonprofit sector that worked with youth. I asked more about it and began to explore more.

Stephen: Was this in Chicago?

Mariana: Yes . . . and so I was eventually hired in child welfare doing case management work. I had an amazing supervisor named Jenny Lopez. She was very quietly motivating and encouraging and educating me about the field. I was working with children in foster care, foster families, biological families. I could tell this was what I wanted to do. This was where I wanted to be. I wanted to be in community, supporting families, looking at policies. Right away, I could see where things were not right. My supervisor encouraged me to get my masters' degree. I remember one time I was on the phone with a client and said I was a social worker. Jenny spoke with me in supervision afterward and told me, "You cannot say you are a social worker unless you have a masters' degree and have a license." I didn't really know about the profession. I went back to school and got my master's degree in social work.

Stephen: You have been in the field for a long time?

Mariana: Yes . . . a long time. Even before that I remember one of my jobs being a court interpreter translating from English to Spanish and Spanish to English, working with judges, attorneys, and lawyers to police officers in lock-up. I was privy to so many systems working together, and I could see where the inequities were.

Stephen: I want to go back to something you said earlier. The experience you shared when you were little in terms of culture and civic engagement . . . learning and understanding your identity in a dominant culture . . . how has that knowledge and connection as a young person influenced you in the work you do in your community.

Mariana: I think it has had a great impact. I haven't talked about my mom, but she is Puerto Rican from New York. She was raised in the foster system in New York. I don't think it was necessarily related to culture and race. Maybe it was, but living in poverty, living in a tragic situation . . . she experienced a lot of trauma at a young age. So knowing that, combined with the information of how Latinos, at that time mostly Mexicans, were treated in the United States, it helped me to think about issues of social justice. I didn't learn any of these things in school. My father talked to us about deportations and repatriations that were happening in California and then during the depression era. I never learned about the history of Mexico, the pyramids, culture, civilizations, and history in Mexico that was not taught in school. He taught me to question the things that were taught or not taught. I learned to be suspicious and more aware, a healthy suspicion, I think. I could have felt more marginalized in terms of who I was, my identity, but I had a pride in where I came from.

I grew up in a neighborhood that was very diverse. I grew up in Austin in the '70s on the West Side of Chicago. I went to school with a large Filipino student population, black, Anglo, Latino, and other immigrant families. There was a mixed income community in Austin. I had a lot of experiences with people different from myself. Those early experience helped me to navigate and begin to understand identity and diversity even though I was so young.

Stephen: It's interesting how so many powerful childhood images and memories have shaped who you are. I wanted to ask a two-part question: How does faith and spirituality play a role in the community you work in? Then how does faith and spirituality influence you personally in the work you do?

Mariana: That's a very interesting question . . . I think that faith and spirituality is very important in the work I do currently. Right now, I am working in a predominantly Latino community. Traditionally, faith has been at the center of that community. In fact, many of the decisions that families make are based on what they believe. Though changing, that religion is primarily Catholic. I think that one of the things I've always been interested in is, from the very beginning of doing child welfare work, was to include that faith, right, by asking questions. You know, do you go to church? Do you believe in something?

Stephen: You mean in terms of reaching out to families?

Mariana: Yes, even though at that time that was not necessarily encouraged. There was research and were professionals in the field who had talked to me about how important understanding faith and spirituality was in the building of relationships with clients. How can you do the work if you don't include a critical part of that person's life? How do you not ask about it? Even today, I have to encourage younger workers to ask families if they go to church . . . Do they have a spiritual support? It's all about being strength-based. For many people, faith and a connection to something greater than themselves is a very real strength and support. So I feel like I've been very open to this, and it has been part of the work.

I have had an interesting experience myself. I was baptized Catholic. My mother converted to Lutheranism, and I went to a Lutheran school for a period. I would say after that, faith was not really a huge part of our lives. My parents were not practicing. My father was not religious in any way. We did not grow up religiously, but what I was able to do was experience many different religions and faiths, mostly Christian religions. I went to Jehovah's Witness churches, Catholic churches, Lutheran churches. I experienced different things, and what it did for me, really couched in my parent's values, was that I didn't like organized religion. It didn't feel very community oriented, how these different faiths wouldn't work with each other. They were isolated. I didn't really connect to any one religion, and as an adolescent, I realized that I just didn't feel connected. As I became an adult, I've always felt connected to a greater power. Not on the religious front but more a spiritual front. As I read more about Native American history, Aztec history, indigenous populations, and the greater connection to the earth, I started to feel differently. I think often and struggle with the image of what God is, this image I was raised with. What could this God be? I think I am actually a little less spiritual, to be honest, than I was even ten years ago.

Stephen: Why is that?

Mariana: I don't know. That's a really good question.

Stephen: That's very interesting. If you don't mind me saying, for someone in your mid-forties, that you were more spiritual ten years ago. What's changed or what's transpired in the last ten years that would pull you away or make you shift that perspective?

Mariana: I think it's being intentional. Unfortunately, I think I have just been less intentional about it. In fact, I've been thinking lately I need to get back to that.

Stephen: Is it fair to say that you feel like you have been a bit spiritually disconnected?

Mariana: Yes, I think so . . . a little bit.

Stephen: I have a tough question . . . Do you believe in a soul? If you do, how would you describe it?

Mariana: Absolutely. I believe in a soul. Do you mean how would I describe a soul?

Stephen: What soul is to you? What does it mean? What does it look like? What does it feel like?

Mariana: That is a very tough question. A deep question. [*Long pause*]

Stephen: You can't pass . . . [*Laughter*]

Mariana: It's interesting you asked me that . . . and that we just had this conversation. I feel like I could have answered that question a lot better ten years ago. When I think of a soul, I think of the deep intelligence and inner workings of the self, you know, what moves us, drives us. Sometimes conscious, sometimes unconscious. This greater internal mission that we are supposed to be doing in life . . . I think that's what I have right now. [*Laughter*]

Stephen: This book has a lot to do with what I call soulfulness, how we bring our soul consciousness present in the world in the work we do and how we interact with people. I know as you are thinking through it . . . do you feel like everyone has access to this type of consciousness? Like the way you described it, that deeper purposefulness, that deeper sense of self whether conscious or unconscious? Do we all have access to that? Are there barriers that exist? Is it given to us by God? What's your thoughts on that?

Mariana: I think that in order to do the work I do, I have to believe that everyone has to have access to it. Are there barriers? Absolutely. I think that in some ways, when you are being soulful, what you are talking about is a level of freedom. In order to get deep into that, there has to be freedom. The capacity to be vulnerable. The capacity to be wrong. Just trying new things in our society, there are so many barriers. History. Poverty. There is always a struggle. Even though people have had a lot of adversity, they still rise and reach their potential. I would be interested to see what that is, how that is accomplished. To be able to get to that place. If we could figure that out, we could probably help a lot of folks, but the reality is there is no one solution. It's many things for many different people. The majority of people, though, can get stuck in those challenges, cycles of poverty, cycles of abuse, cycles of victimization. You almost need a coach to guide you. I see that in my own family, where there are barriers or obstacles in our way. There can be so much potential in someone, but if they can't see them and overcome their barriers, they are just struggling and spinning their wheels.

Stephen: You had said earlier that you were much more of a spiritual person and that you want to find that again. I'm paraphrasing a bit. Do you think that reclaiming some of that spiritual soulfulness and inner connection will elevate the work you do in terms of working with others? I mean, is there a connection there? Your personal connection to a soul and how you connect with other people?

Mariana: I am sure that there is [*Pause*] . . . I would want to say that I'm connecting with people and I am doing real good work, so when I think about this other greater connection, it might help me feel better, feel more free, do work more broadly. I guess I really can't say.

Stephen: It's a hard question.

Mariana: It is . . . Steve . . . you got me thinking. [*Laughter*]

Stephen: I think it feeds our resiliency as a human spirit or human being. Our work is a lot of giving, not a lot of taking. We see a lot of burnout in the field. We see it in our staff. We see it in our community where people get tired of giving back. Your soul needs to be replenished.

That leads me to my next question . . . How do you keep yourself sustained and motivated and energized in a very difficult field that is constantly draining. There's a lot of struggle out there, a lot of challenge.

Mariana: I have a very strong work ethic. I work a lot. That's a value I have and a source of pride. That I am able to do as much as I can with the time I have here. So for me, it is just innate. It's just what I want to do. It's something I value and that I know is valuable to others. But aside from that, I feel like my connection to my family is very important. I was the oldest child. One of the other things that was driven into me was to be the example for your siblings. I still want to be an example. It keeps me going. It keeps me energized. To see what working hard and giving back can do in your life. I want to give back to my community. I feel responsible for that. That when folks get to see me or know me, you can be successful. You can be raised in poverty and still be successful. You can still be happy and give back. The other thing is to always be a learner. Like you don't know everything. People may call me or see me as a leader. I see myself as a learner. In every opportunity, I want to learn and grow. That really keeps me going and to stay connected. Also being able to work closely with the community, in my current role, I see folks come into our center and see what is happening in their lives. Seeing children who have grown up in Family Focus and now are giving back or bringing back their children. It is very rewarding. We actually just hired one of our kids that was in our early childhood program. That is very exciting and rewarding. These are some of the things that feed me.

Stephen: What would you say are one or some of the most memorable outcomes or successes you have had in your career?

Mariana: When I see families be their own advocates and leaders is one of the most powerful things. When parents come in and say they want to develop a parent council, make phone calls about funding issues, or things that are affecting their community. I have seen so many women, primarily women, take on leadership roles at their local school, at our center, believe in themselves, believe they have a story to tell. I think that is very important. It helps to make the work easier because you are able to see new leaders in the field, and they are doing the work in their communities. I've seen parents really begin to understand the field of early childhood. Whereas before, they might say, "Why take my two-year-old to school?" But now, they say, "Yes, I want to get involved in early childhood education. There is a consciousness about learning about what is best for my family and my children. This is primarily with women that may not be making most of the decisions in their home or are not the traditional decision makers but are now making important choices for the development of their children and family.

CHAPTER 16

Learning to Breathe

The moon does not fight. It attacks no one. It does not worry. It does not try to crush others. It keeps to its course, but by its very nature, it gently influences. What other body could pull an entire ocean from shore to shore? The moon is faithful to its nature and its power is never diminished.
—Deng Ming-Dao

In 1996, I met Grandmaster Key Chun Song, a doctor of acupuncture and herbal medicine, qigong healing and meditation as well as a teacher of tai chi chuan and hsing-i chuan, two internal styles of Chinese martial arts. In my journey of studying Chinese martial arts and Taoist philosophy with Grandmaster Song, I have learned many, many things. Having achieved a rank of fifth Dan and title of Sifu, or master, has been a great honor and achievement both personally and spiritually. However, one of the most important elements of my teaching has been recognizing the fact that we are on a path of continual learning. No title, no ranking, and no level of experience allows us to say that we have completed the learning journey. In fact, I have come to realize very clearly through martial arts that the more I know, the more I have to learn.

In 2011, I was asked by a close friend Sam Chaltain, a brilliant academic, educator, and author, as well as the writer of the foreword of this book, to write a short chapter for a work called *Faces of Learning*. In his book, various individuals were asked to write about a unique learning experience, specifically answering the following two questions:

1. What was your most powerful personal experience in a learning community—regardless of whether it took place inside or outside of school?
2. Who was your most effective teacher, and what was it about that person that made him or her so effective?

I chose to write about Key Chun Song for multiple reasons but ultimately because of the profound impact he has made on my life. Many aspects of my learning and growth through meditation and martial arts have informed my professional career, marriage, role as a father, a friend, human being and ultimately put me on a path toward better understanding my spiritual self and reaching toward my own understanding of the concept and idea of finding soul consciousness.

Excerpt from *Faces of Learning*

2011

I sat quietly on the floor with my legs crossed. We listened attentively to our teacher as he stood still like a mountain, aged with experience and wisdom. My classmates and I took in every word and motion as he taught ancient methods for the most basic of human actions: respiration—inhale and exhale. If you were not in the class, you might find it odd, ten students sitting crossed-legged behind glass walls that separated us from the hustle and horns of busy buses, cars and passers-by on the Northwest Side of Chicago.

Key Chun Song is in his late sixties, short and well groomed. His white collared sleeves are rolled once, showing his strong forearms. His face is calm and peaceful, with high cheekbones and a wisp of a mustache and goatee. He is short in stature, but gives no impression of weakness. He is solid like a tree trunk, roots sunk deep into the earth. He is unlike any teacher I have ever had. He speaks in broken English, yet I understand him clearly through his subtle metaphors. Maybe it is the many years I have listened to his voice, but I can easily pick out the words he stumbles over. It seems that traditional teachers, those I have had throughout my Western education, do a lot of talking, force-feeding the material.

Somehow, in the years I have studied under Grandmaster Song, I have realized that less is more. Just as we must relearn to breathe deeply as when we were infants, expanding the abdomen . . . filling our entire chest . . . we must relearn learning. How can one explore and learn creatively? Through action and experience, reflecting and revisiting—not being graded on false markers or others predetermined expectations—passing or failing.

I sit quietly on the floor. Inhale and exhale. My shoulders and back are relaxed. My head and spine are erect, as if being held up by a string. I am calm and peaceful, following the gentle words of my teacher. A smile is lightly present on my face, the same as the nine other students in the class. I am a baby, learning to breathe.

This short story that reflects on my teacher and a class on learning to meditate and breathe is an excellent analogy to relearning how to connect with our soul consciousness. We must cleanse ourselves of the bias, hate, prejudice, pain, and fear we have learned over our life journey. We must find a way to fortify our ability to live our life with love, honesty, integrity, and wonder. Just as we have forgotten how to breathe effectively, filling the lung cavity and fully oxygenating our blood to fortify our cells and physical body, we must relearn how to connect with our spiritual selves, to other spirits, and to find our soul's purpose in our physical and spiritual journey on this earth.

The work of personal development and spiritual grounding is deeply connected to the work of community empowerment and creating an opportunity for systemic change. As Roberto Rivera eloquently shares in an earlier chapter, "Our souls are like a patchwork quilt, waiting to be stitched together by our shared consciousness and collective purpose." I hope we as a community, a nation, and world can soon begin that work.

Chapter 17

Volney "VP" Parker

Little Rock, Arkansas

You can search throughout the entire universe for someone who is more deserving of your love and affection than you are yourself, and that person is not to be found anywhere. You yourself, as much as anybody in the entire universe deserve your love and affection.

—Buddha

VP Parker is someone I call a brother from another mother. We have known each other for over fifteen years and had an opportunity to travel across the United States together. We worked on various government and non-government contracts together and built a strong relationship and friendship. I think I am most thankful to VP for his mentorship and guidance in our work with diversity and inclusion strategies for communities, nonprofits, and Fortune 500 companies. His insight, passion, and knowledge for the elevation of these topics as it pertained to issues of human interaction, capacity building, and even financial ROI for the likes of Johnson & Johnson and Abercrombie & Fitch was really phenomenal. He helped me to become an external consultant with the premier minority-owned D&I firm in the United States at the time, Global Lead, and helped to develop my skills and talents in working with corporate leadership and having them understand the depth of purpose, meaning, and financial benefit to embrace issues of inclusion not only for their workforce but also for their external market and operational success. Over the years, we had the opportunity to watch each other's family and children grow and have stayed connected. While having come from different backgrounds, cultures, and geographic locations in the United States, we both happened to have married outside of our own ethnic group, raised biracial children, and have understood the role inclusivity, understanding of one's history, and the divisive nature of our American culture has played out in our society. VP's commitment to challenging the status quo, forcing those of us willing to look beyond our reflection and deep into the mirror of the soul, has inspired me greatly in my journey both as an educator and human being.

Stephen: Tell me a little about yourself, a bit about your background, and the work you do in communities.

VP: My name is Volney Parker. People call me VP, and my background is Creole. I didn't realize this until I was eight or nine, so I really grew up black. The reason why this is important is because of the work I do in the community. It's usually around inclusiveness, multiculturalism, pluralism, and cultural competence. So that's how I see myself.

Stephen: As Creole?

VP: Yes, but I also see myself as someone who is trying to elevate the discussion around dismantling of oppression and elevating my own personal awareness. For those people who want to hear what I have to say, hopefully elevating their own personal awareness to where we are doing things differently, and I don't mean on a big scale. I just mean on the day to day. How we interact with our kids, how we see ourselves, or how we help other people or be supportive of them when they're fighting oppression. I don't just mean that from a minority perspective. I mean anybody who is alive and while you are being affected by some systems that either oppress or affect you in some way. I think MLK said, "If one person is being affected we are all being affected." I am a father. I take that very seriously. I am a spouse, and I take that seriously. I've got five kids. Who am I? I am a dad trying to live a life where I don't really know exactly what dads are supposed to do because I didn't grow up with one, but I am trying to live a life like when they become parents, they will say I kind of want to do it like him.

Stephen: I have to back up a second. First of all, can you explain for people what is Creole for those who may not know and what that means to you.

VP: Creole is an ethnicity or a subset of an ethnicity. It is a mixture of French and Indian, more specifically black French. My Indian tribe is Choctaw. I know this because one of my cousins, my first cousin in New Orleans, did the research.

Stephen: You grew up in New Orleans?

VP: No, I grew up in Little Rock, Arkansas. I've grown to visit New Orleans with my family and still have uncles and cousins there. My first cousin did the research and did the genealogy on it. We went back to knowing our black French ancestors are from France and have pictures from who our Choctaw matriarch is. He went way back, which is awesome. I own that. I didn't grow up in New Orleans, but I'm claiming that. I love it. I love the history of it. I love everything that having those roots are all about.

Stephen: That just made me think of another thing to go back to. Obviously, with the work you said you do, working on diversity, dealing with oppression, and understanding self, you have obviously connected to your roots and your history, but you also said you grew up without your dad. How does that play into the work you do, or does it? Looking at the work you do, does it play a role . . . or even a role in looking at your own history?

VP: I bet it has a role. I'm not exactly sure what the role is explicitly. I know it has a role because of the young people I have worked with in leadership roles or work I have done in nonprofit organizations. I am a voice for them. Right now, I am in Boys' State.

Stephen: What did you say, a what?

VP: Boys State. It is a leadership civic organization, usually sponsored by the American Legion. What they do is bring together youth leadership of Boys' and Girls' State, and they are usually together for a week. They learn how the civic system works. It is life changing. I came from a family of a lot of Boys' Staters. It was life changing for me.

Stephen: Interesting. I've never heard of this before up here in Chicago. Do they have a chapter up here?

VP: I bet they do. I bet there is one in every State. Now that I go back, the people who run it in the state of Arkansas ask me to come back every year and speak to the group of boys. I feel a sense of kinship because I had the same experience, but some of the things I impart to them is coming from a fatherly place. So they already have dads. Most of them if not all of them. But I still feel I need to impart something to them as if I was a father.

Stephen: Well, you are. You have five kids.

VP: That's true, but I didn't grow up with one. I don't know what the model is. Like I saw other kids with fathers. They would come to school and do father things. I didn't have that. I don't think I ever felt that as a loss. I never felt that way. My mother was a single mother of three. I was the middle of three children, and she was fantastically awesome in providing everything we felt that we needed. There was very little we felt wanting for, even though we were [*pause*] dirt poor. We were impoverished, but that same song you may hear impoverished people say, "We didn't know we were poor." She never complained about my dad not being around. It was never an issue. My father died when I was very young. Really young. I did not have the opportunity to meet him or know him. There's no baseline for what I am supposed to do. I am trying to set a high bar for myself. The kids I have are unbelievable kids. I know that is biased, but . . .

Stephen: What are their ages?

VP: Let's see . . . a twenty-three-year-old, a thirteen-year-old, an eleven-year-old who will soon be twelve, a nine-year-old girl, and an eight-year-old girl. Three boys and two girls.

Stephen: That's a lot . . . That's a big family.

VP: That's a lot, a lot . . . and I have a spouse, my wife.

Stephen: Dog . . . cat . . . [*laughter*]

VP: [*Laughter*] I got two dogs . . . Here's the thing, though, especially after we visited your house . . . my wife so badly wants chickens.

Stephen: Oh, we got rid of those chickens last year.

VP: I'm glad to hear it . . . She's pushing for those chickens. So we had a conversation and she said, "For my birthday, I want chickens."

I said, "Babe, I'm just not down with that." We live in downtown Little Rock!

Stephen: Do you have a backyard?

VP: We have a small backyard. It's super small. Whatever you are thinking small right now, go half of that, and it's even smaller.

Stephen: You can fly me to Little Rock, and I can build you a chicken coop.

VP: Well . . . I don't have space . . . [*laughter*]. Because I wasn't down with the chickens, we bought another dog.

Stephen: We digress. [*Both laughing*] Let me go back to your work with dismantling oppression. Can you give me the context of your work. What do you do? Who do you do it with and where?

VP: Sure . . . ever since 1990, I have been doing trainings and workshops on multiculturalism and cultural competence, and then in the mid- and late-'90s, I went into anti-ism trainings. Really, that's the bottom line. How we look at the systems that create oppression for people and how those systems affect people and create the disparities we have now. The next step once we understand and know it is how do we go about eradicating it. That's not something you can do in a workshop. It's a constant ongoing conversation, and then you have to live it, or at least try to live it. Later, I transitioned this work into the corporate world. Talking about the same material, just in a different context. In the realm of inclusive leadership of being a transformational leader and how we must see things differently by changing the cultural and behavior of an organization when it may not be set up to support all people within that organization.

Stephen: Basically, you have your own consulting business.

VP: Absolutely, that's correct. I have had that since 1990 and work with several Fortune 500 companies and have done and still do work with international consulting firms. Even now I am working with the military, teaching and instructing military officers in organizational leadership.

Stephen: Do you travel a lot?

VP: I used to travel a lot when I was working for the consulting firm full-time. I was traveling probably 75 percent of the time. Not as much anymore. I had a conversation with my wife, and she asked me . . . Well, she didn't ask me. She told me—

Stephen: To do some more local shit! [*Laughter*]

VP: She said, and I'll put it out exactly how she said it to me, "I didn't sign up for this."

"For what?" I said."

She said, "I did not sign up to be a single, married parent." She was exactly right. We have a lot of kids at home. I was on the road too much.

Stephen: That totally makes sense . . . So what keeps you motivated in your field and the work you do?

VP: I cannot get enough of learning. That's what drives me. I always want to know more, learn the next thing. Because I consistently have a stage and people to speak in front of, I want to have new information to share. What's the newest thing, the connections to be made that no one has put together before.

Also, what sustains me is trying to make this place better for my kids. When you have little ones, you want to leave this world a little better. I've got four little ones and a twenty-three-year-old. I've got five kids, so what can I do to make this place better than it was when they were born?

Stephen: This book has a definite spiritual slant to it. I wanted to ask you about your own religious beliefs or spirituality, your faith, however that may look or not look and whether it may play a role in the work that you do?

VP: I have an interesting experience when it comes to faith, religion, and spirituality. I grew up in the South, in the Bible belt. It was understood that everyone went to church, and we did. We did go to church, my brother and I. He's two years older than me. The part that's interesting to me is, my grandmother, the matriarch of our family, she is COGIC. Church of God in Christ. Very expressive when they worship. They have the drums, they've got the piano, the organ, the choir. They have the stereotypical black church you see on TV. They have the over-the-top comedic type stuff, like folks running up and down the aisle, talking to the Holy Ghost.

Stephen: Like in *The Blues Brothers* movie.

VP: Absolutely, absolutely . . . This is the church I went to every Sunday since the day I was born. What brings people together is church. Black folks are brought together by church. This was not an integrated church. My grandmother was the head usher. She's been in that spot for a long time, Lily Pearl Gatewood. She was amazing. She would take us to Sunday school at seven forty-five or eight. Then we would be taken to church till about 2:00 p.m. That's a long time. Then we would be fellowshipping for a few hours and then back to 6:00 p.m. worship. All day. Now my grandfather who has been married to my grandmother for fifty-five years goes to a different church. The AME church . . . African Methodist Episcopal Church. Totally different. 180.

Stephen: More reserved.

VP: Oh, man . . . methodical, hymn books. Everyone sings together. Stands up and sits down together. They talked about the holy spirit, but no one was running up and down the aisle catching the Holy Ghost. The pulpit was for the pastor . . . That's it. My grandfather was a key figure for over forty years. What I am saying is my experience with religion was early on. There was definitely nobody but Jesus, but just the dichotomy of these two systems did a great job in setting me up for the idea that . . . both of these churches were praising the same God, just doing it differently . . . and there were conversations about who was doing a better job, yet they were praising the same God. Same Jesus.

Stephen: Did you feel part of the systems. Did you believe in the religion and the belief systems? Do you know what I mean? Or were you just a passive participant?

VP: I absolutely felt a part of it because there was no other option. No one stood over me and said, "You better believe." I'm not saying that. It's just that if you are brought up in church and that's all you know . . . then that's all you know. Somehow or another, my family, my mother, grandparents, aunts, and uncles, they were . . . I don't ever remember them telling me that if "you don't believe, you are going to hell." Not that I didn't pick up on it. That just comes along with the organized religion. I'm now at a point with my faith that it's not as dogmatic as when I was growing up. Faith and spirituality and one's personal faith is just that, personal. No matter how much a doctrine or a dogma or ideology tells you that this is how it is or how it should be, and you will fall short of the glory of God. I now realize that this is the number 1 reason young and middle-aged people are moving away from organized religion. It's too confining. It's putting you in a box. If you are going to preach to me that God is big, omnipotent, and omniscient, then how can God put us in a box. I don't subscribe to that anymore. I subscribe to something different. There is one God, and everybody calls him something different. I am not in a position to tell anybody that they are wrong. I am a Christian, but I can totally connect with all other religions because it's bigger than me. My faith, my prayer, my meditation is enough to motivate me.

Stephen: You have a lot of consistency in terms of inclusivity in your work, your personal relationship, your belief system in that the spiritual domain, the personal domain, and the professional domain are all places that honor inclusion and diversity, which is interesting in itself. My question is, though, how did you become this way? Do you have any insight on that? It's a theme throughout your life.

VP: I already shared that my grandparents were praising the same God but from a different Christian faith tradition, I think that was a factor. There was this one teacher, her name was Ms. Brown. Fourth grade teacher. While she taught us how to add, subtract, divide, read and spell, unbeknown to us, she was feeding us wonderful, wonderful stuff about getting along with people who are unlike you.

Stephen: She was intentional about it?

VP: Yes, she was very intentional. We did not know what she was doing.

Stephen: Was it a diverse classroom?

VP: Mostly black and white. What she did was teach us some things that leveraged what was inside of us. She took that and tripled it or cubed it, but when we look back on it now, she was ahead of her time. She instilled in us a mind-set of inclusivity that was unique. I know her now and talk with her and let her know how much of a role she played in my life. We all learned to lean on each other, check each other, count on each other. This was fourth grade all the way to high school. The last thing was that my family, mother, grandparents, and aunts never told me I was wrong for being around a diverse group of people unlike me. They always said be cautious, but they never stopped me from connecting with people who were different from me.

Stephen: I am going to take us back to the spiritual side of things. Maybe a deeper part of this book I am writing. Do you believe in a soul? If so, what does the concept of a soul look like in your mind? I know that's a big question.

VP: Yeah, it is . . . I do believe in a soul. I am trying to figure out where to start. Here is what I think the soul is. I think that, however humanity started . . . there was a Creator. I'm going to call that God, with the understanding that other people may call that Creator something different. So I'm not trying to be narrow-minded or narrowly focused. God, when creating humanity, there was nothing but a soul. It was spiritual, transparent. It had no other attributes other than what God is. This soul did not have anything mortal attached to it, but when we became human beings, the soul needed something to protect it. An outer shell, a human shell, that's what these bodies we are walking around in. Inside is where the soul lives. It is always looking to connect or reconnect with people that are around, which is why I think intrinsically or inherently we are always looking to connect with people. We cannot survive by ourselves. What drives that, scientists would say, is biology, but I think it's the soul saying, "I've got something inside of me that wants to connect and look to connect." Our mortal bodies and our brain and conditioning is always trying to keep us from connecting. The soul is the part inside of us that is saying, "I want to be connected to the Creator, and as a part of being connected to the Creator, I am also connected to you. It doesn't matter what faith you believe in. Everyone has a soul regardless of faith. That being the case, it always is easier to connect with people who look like you, act like you, and talk like you. Your soul always wants to connect with people and that's cool, but your soul gets an even bigger high when you connect with someone who's not like you. Or who doesn't look like you, talk like you, dance like you, eat the same food as you. The only reason I think the soul relishes in that even more is that the soul realizes that in order to have created that relationship, it took more of your soul to do it. It took more of your soul. It was invested in it. Is it all right that I talk about soul consciousness?

Stephen: That's actually part of the title of this book.

VP: That's good. I think that the soul has a consciousness.

Stephen: You mean the soul itself, outside of our brain and physical body?

VP: Absolutely. That consciousness is the need to connect. Now there is a consciousness that we can have about our soul and . . . Let me ask you, is that where your book goes?

Stephen: Am I being interviewed now? [*Laughter*]

VP: Yes, you are. [*Laughter*] Is your book and writing about the moral consciousness of the soul, or the consciousness we can have about our soul?

Stephen: I think it's both. Can I give you an answer?

VP: Absolutely, please.

Stephen: I think there is an element of this where I want people to become more conscious of a soul and the souls we possess, but that's at the surface level. The deeper level is what you described. The oneness that I believe we are trying or should be trying to get to through our soul connection. So the innate connection you have to me as a human being is not because of our skin color or our physical environment or our upbringing. It's from something deeper. So in answering your question, it's both, a consciousness of the soul and then tapping into what that means in understanding our own soul consciousness and spiritual connection to others.

VP: You first asked me if I believe in a soul. I want to back up and share with you why I think the answer was yes. Not only is it because we are connected to a Creator but also when I think about how we use the word "soul" . . . here are some of the way we use it . . . soul brother, soul mate, touched my soul, I can feel it in my soul, soul music, warm soup for the soul, soothes the soul. All these things are really getting to something that we don't often think about which is, all the things I just mentioned have to do with your soul being touched in a way that was deeper than any of the superficial mortal stuff. When someone says their soul was touched, they are saying there has been a profound, euphoric, transcendent touching. When someone says soul mate, it's not because we think alike or that we look alike. It's a whole other level. Like the concept of an old soul. The implication of how we use the word "soul" reminds me, whether people want to admit it or not, that our souls are very conscious of trying to connect with other people because of how we use the words. That's a wonderful thing. I think our souls are what drives us to do the things that are best truly for humanity.

Stephen: I was thinking about a comment you made earlier . . . about wanting to leave things better for your children than when you got here. I am starting to connect a little bit more in what you are saying now in relation to the work you do. How we connect with one another and how one of the purposes, as I am doing these interviews and understanding this work more, is how we connect with one another's souls is truly about making that deeper purposeful change. Part of what I have begun to understand in thinking about and writing this is the correlation between the people in this book, for example, and how profound their work is to them personally but also spiritually. How this concept of soul touching is about really connecting with people and communities on a much deeper level. The part I have been really struggling with is the reality we see in our communities across the country and around the world: the pain, the poverty, the violence, the inequity. That's what I struggle with. I'm not sure that is a question or just me rambling.

VP: Let me tell you something. Let me tell you something. I'm going to read this quote. I usually have this memorized because it's so powerful. The part that you said you are struggling with of where we are right now. I share this with myself so that I remember that I am the one who is in charge of making things change. I can't put it on anyone else. I can't blame it on the system, on colonialism, or Columbus, whatever. But in the here and now, what can I do. Here is the quote. I usually do this from memory on stage. It's from Haim Ginott, teacher, parent educator, and psychologist. "I have come to the frightening conclusion that I am the decisive element. It is my personal approach that creates the climate, it is my daily mood that makes the weather. I possess tremendous power to make life miserable or joyous. I can be a tool of torture or instrument of inspiration. I can humiliate, humor, hurt or heal. In every situation, it is my response that decides whether a crisis is escalated or de-escalated and whether a person is humanized or dehumanized. If we treat people as they are we make them worse. If we treat them as they ought to be we help them become what they are capable of becoming." Just the first line, "I have come to the frightening conclusion that I am the decisive element." We can spend an entire interview on this line. Why is it frightening? It's frightening because I am the one responsible. It's on me that I approach the world in a way that says, "What have I done?" "How can I change it to make it better?" "How can I communicate differently?" "How can I help influence the people around me?" It's an uphill battle for you and me, anyone who is in this line of work. It took hundreds and hundreds of years to get here. We're not going to change it in fifty years, but did you try? The question is, did you try?

CHAPTER 18

A Final Thought

When one door of happiness closes, another opens; but often we look so long at the closed door that we do not see the one which has been opened for us.
—Helen Keller

Through my writing and participation in the interview process for this book over the last few years, I have come to understand how, for some, the individual personal journey, professional career, and spiritual path is inextricably linked and intertwined with the journey of the communities within which the individual serves. Communities are living organisms— dynamic, evolving, and made up of the sum of its parts. We must learn to walk through this world with a conscious desire for connection and spiritual purpose if we want to manifest change in our communities. A soulful purpose and conscious mind, however, is not enough to make systemic changes. All those interviewed in this book will tell you that the work of empowerment and community change takes struggle and persistence. It takes patience and a tireless commitment to people and the belief in their ability to grow, learn, and exercise their own innate ability to bring out what is best within them.

This type of internal focus, passion, and belief in oneself and belief in the ability of others must also be paired with sound policies, thoughtful leadership, intentional actions, a commitment to social justice, and real economic opportunities for those that have been disenfranchised. There must be trust in our local and grassroots leaders and their ability to be harbormasters and agents of change and transformation. In order to begin this process of change, there has to be a philosophical and spiritual shift in our society, a shift in our unique American identity and human consciousness. A true understanding of equity and equality begins with a deep reflective look at our individual and collective history as Americans. At the same time, there must also be an inner understanding and authentic connection to the self. This connection to the self is manifested by an authentic understanding and relationship to our soul and our deeper purpose. We have to be open and embrace an awakening of our spirit, binding us to one another as never before in our human history, but this will only happen if we are willing to listen deeply to the inner voice that speaks to us with confidence and clarity. It is a voice from the source of all things and of all things. We have to calm the fear of our conscious mind and open our heart to listen with intention and purpose.

My desire is that through these stories, experiences, life learnings, and reflections that are written within these pages, we can walk away from this book with a deeper knowledge and understanding of the incredible work that is being done locally and across the country. More importantly, how each of our soul's purpose informs, guides, and leads our effectiveness and impact. How overcoming our personal challenges and pain is a roadmap for overcoming our larger societies' illnesses. The beautiful and powerful people that illuminate this book with their stories are at the core of its purpose and meaning. Through these conversations and interviews, we can hopefully be guided to a deeper and more conscious connection to one another. A more conscious purpose that elevates our collective humanity and brings deeper opportunities for the social changes we so desperately desire. A hopeful spiritual awakening that has the power to transform and reshape our society and indeed the world we know.

Soul Consciousness

A New Vision of Community Empowerment and Cultural Transformation

Interview Questions

1. Tell me about who you are, where you came from, and the work you do in your community.
2. What sustains you and keeps you motivated?
3. How does faith play a role in your community and your work?
4. Do you believe in a soul? If so, how would you describe it?
5. What are your greatest challenges and barriers to success?
6. How do we create large-scale, sustainable community impact and change?
7. How do you view the relationship between your personal and professional journey?
8. How would you describe leadership in your community?
9. What helps you to stay committed during challenging times?
10. How can communities access resources needed for programmatic impact?
11. Can you share an example of positive change and growth in your community?
12. What are some of the critical factors for successful community collaboration?
13. What keeps you resilient, hopeful, and optimistic?

Anndrea Miller   Volney "VP" Parker   Loren Fardulis

Antwan Diggs   Mariana Osoria   Teh' Ray "Phenom" Hale Sr.

Jewel Ware   Roberto Rivera   Charles Perry